MRS. GROSSMAN'S
STICKER MAGIC

MRS. GROSSMAN'S
STICKER MAGIC

Andrea Grossman
and Leslie Conron Carola

HUGH LAUTER LEVIN ASSOCIATES, INC.

ISBN-10: 0-88363-707-3
ISBN-13: 978-0-88363-707-4

An Arena Books Associates Book
Book concept and development: Leslie Conron Carola,
Arena Books Associates, LLC
Design: Kathleen Herlihy-Paoli, Inkstone Design, Inc.
Photography: Jon Van Gorder

From Leslie C. Carola: It has been my great joy to work with Andrea Grossman, an extraordinary woman who brings the magic (with and without stickers) to everyone.

ACKNOWLEDGMENTS
Thank you to the following artists who have created the art projects:
Kelly Carolla, Sandi Genovese, Andrea Grossman,
Amy Jill Wallace, Barb Wendel.

Special thanks to the people who design the stickers, making the magic possible: Julie Cohen, Audrey Georgi, Tami Lovett-Brumfield,
and Gigi Sproul.

Thanks to Tracey Trumbo for providing the project
technical information.

Additional thanks to Shannon Aja, Raul Chacon, Kevin Dunlop,
and Leslie Randle.

And thank you to Sherryl Kumli for keeping every ball
in the air at all times.

The names of all Mrs. Grossman's Paper Company products have registered trademarks. We did not include the symbols throughout the book in the interest of simplicity, but they are listed here and are so protected. They include: Accents Too ™, Design Lines[R], Extravagant™, Photoessence[R], Paper Whispers[R], Reflections™, Stickers by the Yard [R] Sticky Patches™, Sticker Stackers™, Textured Tags™.

If stickers are unavailable at your local craft store, log onto mrsgrossmans.com and follow the link for *Mrs. Grossman's Sticker Magic*.

CONTENTS

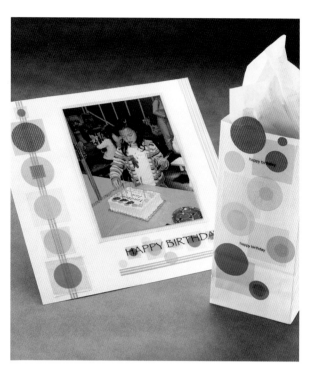

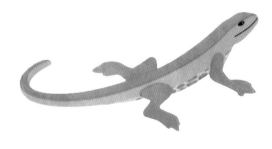

INTRODUCTION

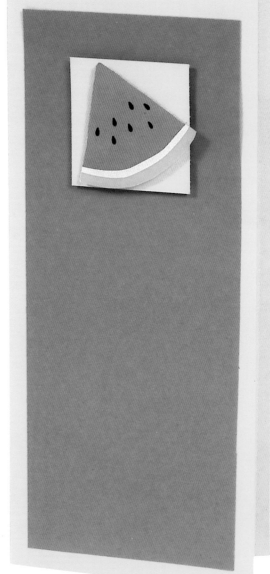

When is a sticker much more than a simple sticker? When it is a Mrs. Grossman's sticker, of course! Not only are Mrs. Grossman's stickers made for each other, made to work together, to make designing a project with them easy, but they are made to encourage you and keep your creative possibilities open. Whether you are five years old or twenty-five, or fifty or a hundred years old, you can enjoy creating sticker art—from delightful colorful projects with and for children to subtle, sophisticated projects for the most elegant occasions.

Gathering some fundamentals of design before setting out to create your own sticker art projects will help to develop your creative intuition. Learn to trust your own eye to tell you what works and what doesn't work. Before starting on a project think about the following: What is the project for? Who or what are you celebrating? What do you want to say, and what response do you want to elicit? Are you going to use just a few stickers arranged in a pleasing composition or are you creating a scene with many stickers? The process is really the same. If you place just one sticker on a card, you want to place it in the most advantageous spot, to elicit a specific response. Even when you want to create a simple design, though, you might use two or three stickers. Choose your palette well. The charming watermelon sticker card (right) is very simple, and powerful. The message sings summer from the contrasting dark and light greens to the slice of ripe watermelon casually balanced at an angle over the light green square. The composition is centered horizontally, but off-centered vertically. The equal border of dark green on either side and above the matted watermelon promotes a feeling of confidence. We feel centered.

Pleasing rhythms, harmonious colors, and balanced compositions are the basic ingredients of good design. There

are two kinds of balance to consider in your designs: symmetrical and asymmetrical. Symmetrical balance is stable and structured, bringing a graceful order to a layout. The *25 Popped Hearts* card (right) with stickers created by Andrea Grossman for the twenty-fifth anniversary of the company is a classic symmetric design: each heart is centered in its own square, and the five-by-five square grid is centered on the card. The palette is harmonious and pleasing. The hearts are elevated from the card surface with foam tape. We love to add interest to our proj-

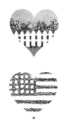

ects by lifting a few of the elements off the page, adding depth and shadow. One of our favorite techniques, "popping" is simple to execute and it makes a strong impact.

Symmetrical compositions offer a classic quality, one found in most formal wedding invitations, for example. A symmetrical design is usually the same on each side of a center line, although it can be modified. Symmetrical balance can be achieved with elements that are not exactly the same on either side of center, as long as they occupy the same visual space on the layout. The composition of the little red gift bag (left) is not exactly the same on either side of center, but the blossoms occupy the same

Create grand sticker art by combining dramatic colors, textures, and stickers.

visual space and successfully balance each other. Balance that is asymmetrical brings contrast, excitement, and motion to a layout. Asymmetrical design often requires a bit more planning than a straightforward symmetrical one, but the extra effort can produce imaginative results. Shifting the focal point and embellishments off center is one way to create asymmetrical balance, as in the elegant gatefold card with the torn off-center edge on the opposite page.

The image below presents the components used in creating one of our favorite Asian-inspired boxes from the group shown opposite the title page. These are

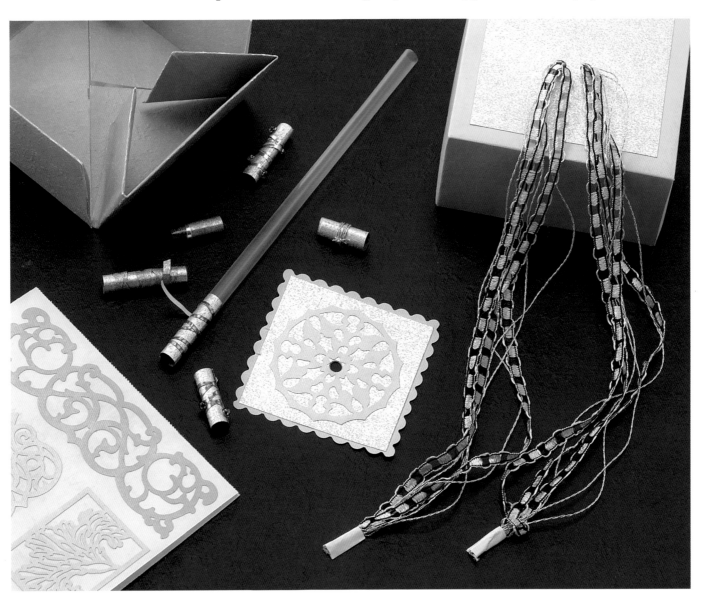

the pieces to a not-very-difficult but gorgeous puzzle. The combination of a subdued palette and simple geometric shapes with the tantalizing ribbon textures is irresistible. Notice that we used sections of a drinking straw to create sticker-wrapped beads on the decorative ribbon.

It's easy to create effective designs when you combine and position stickers on a card. By grouping sticker images you create visual order—a focal point—in your picture. Then the space around and between the stickers (negative space) brings attention to the stickered image (focal point). We love the soft, natural effect of handmade paper. The tulip bowl card (right) combines mulberry paper with stickers. This well-composed card with a centered design is about texture and tone—layers of soft, thready texture with a soft, unifying palette. A second set of tulip stickers layered just off-center over the first ones adds intriguing depth and shading.

When you are starting out creating sticker art, work out your layout on scrap paper before sticking everything down on your card, scrapbook page, or gift wrap.

♥

ADD SHADOW AND DEPTH TO A LAYOUT, BY PLACING ONE STICKER FLAT ON A CARD OR PANEL AND THEN ADDING A SECOND STICKER (THE SAME IMAGE) SLIGHTLY OFF-CENTER ON TOP OF THE ORIGINAL ONE. BE SURE TO PLACE A SMALL PIECE OF MOUNTING TAPE BENEATH THE SECOND STICKER TO LIFT IT OFF THE SURFACE.

♥

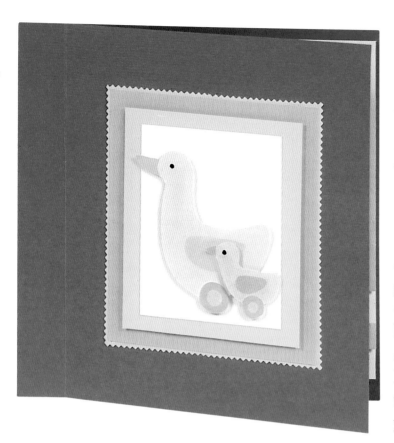

And, build your sticker scenes on sticker backing paper before attaching them to your finished project. A simple scene could be built right on your fingertip , but it is safer to construct a scene on the sticker backing paper before transferring it to your card.

Stickers are so much more than you think. Kids have always loved them, and so do adults. You can do anything with stickers. Want to create a gift album of new baby photos for grandmother (like the one at left)? Want to decorate a bag or box, or spark a reaction? Make fabulous, sophisticated invitations to a black-tie dinner party? Haven't had time to call a distant friend? Break the ice and the silence, renew the friendship: send your best sticker art—a card or note.

How do you start? Jump right in and make a card for someone you love—a spouse, a parent, a grandparent, brother or sister, a friend, a teacher, a son or daughter, niece or nephew, uncle or aunt. Do something from your heart. A handmade card or simple gift from you will brighten the day of anyone you love.

Whether a quiet one- or two-sticker arrangement on a card, or an elaborate, fun-filled scene with many stickers, let your art speak for you. Like the spirited album at right, count your blessings and celebrate life.

SUPPLIES NEEDED TO CREATE STICKER ART

BASIC SUPPLIES

Scissors; craft knife; personal trimmer; pointed tweezers; ruler; adhesives (glue stick, double stick tape, dry line); powder & brush; pencil; black, gold and silver pens; mounting tape; cutting mat; eraser; bone folder

PAPERS

Blank cards in a variety of colors; embossed cardstocks – we have used Mrs. Grossman's Scrapbook Symmetry papers because of their colors and textures, and we love tearing them, leaving a dramatic white edge; colored cardstocks in soft and bright shades; sheer, metallic, and pearl vellum (Mrs. Grossman's are colored to coordinate with Scrapbook Symmetry papers); metal sheets (Etal) and metallic coated papers.

ADDITIONAL SUPPLIES

Paper punches; die cuts; gold and silver cord; gold, silver and colored wires; monofilament; decorative fibers; ribbons; decorative-edge scissors; metal brads, eyelets and embellishments; acetate, stamp pads; pigment powder; colored pencils, chalk; craft lacquer; fixative spray.

LUGGAGE TAGS

How to tell your black bag from all the others on the baggage-claim carousel? Make your own luggage tags! And then make individualized luggage tags as Christmas gifts for everyone in your family and all your friends this year. Imagine a baggage carousel filled with bright, cheerful colors that would make anyone smile. Our high-top sneaker tags would work for any traveling athlete. And as for the traveling dog tags—these canines will go in style. What fun. These tags go straight to the heart of Mrs. Grossman's sticker art fun. They demonstrate composed scenes with an established horizon line, with stickers in the background and foreground, and stickers cut to fit their spots (look at the little pup and the tickets in the rear suitcase, and the bones in the Scottie's suitcase pocket). Start with the background first, and work forward. The background images are further away and a little higher on the page than the foreground images.

BALLOON SHOPPING BAG CARD

Clean, bright colors, whimsical sticker images, and a sense of fun are all you need to make us all want to float away on a summer's day breeze. The coordinated palette is bright, the simple composition is centered, and the cheery balloon stickers are layered and popped with foam mounting tape.

LAYERING & POPPING

One sticker alone on a page can be stunning. Layer one sticker on top of another, and it is very appealing. Layer again onto another, and you have something special. Then try elevating one or two of the stickers (or a mat) off the page surface with small pieces of mounting tape underneath, and you have something magical. The humble sticker takes on a new life. It is a whole new world.

We love to create scenes with stickers. And Mrs. Grossman's stickers are made for each other. They are made to work together, so designing a project with them is easy, and the creative possibilities limitless. Whether or not you create actual "scenes" is up to you, but do get in the habit of layering two or more stickers together in a pleasing composition to create interesting dimension.

Most of Mrs. Grossman's stickers are printed as mirror images—identical shapes facing opposite directions—to allow you greater freedom in creating sticker art. You can "finish" your art on two sides if you place one sticker off the edge of a card, and then place its mirror image back-to-back with it off the reverse of the card.

Think about textures and backgrounds. You have so many choices. Colorful or monochromatic contrasting papers add texture. Overlap some stickers and you have created texture and depth. Lift some papers and stickers off the page with mounting tape and you have textured layers of increased dimension.

One of the design elements we are most interested in is the space left around a stickered image or scene. The sticker shape itself is the positive space. The space left around the sticker is the negative space. Negative space is as important a design element as any sticker itself. It spotlights the main attraction. Please don't feel compelled to fill every space. Think of the action on stage in the theater. Isolate the focal point—the main character—and arrange the supporting characters in a pleasing or dramatic way. Present *your* design onstage. Make sure the focal point is well positioned, and showcased. Think of the negative space as breathing room. Without it you can smother a scene with too many stickers. With it, your sticker images will glow in the spotlight.

BOX TOWERS

Birthdays are meant for celebration: bright colors, fireworks, candles, polka dots, and piles of presents rise to the occasion. These jubilant towers of boxes celebrate any special occasion—birthday, Christmas, or the New Year. It is an appealing way to present gifts. And, of course, the tower of varying sized boxes adds to the intrigue and mystery. Are the gifts related? Does one lead to the next? Are the different color boxes significant? One could wonder and wonder about this presentation.

For the summer birthday tower, select three bright-colored square boxes. Place firework stickers on the box sides, and then add solid mats of yellow, violet, or blue topped with white panels decorated with candles and balloons floating off the edges. A multicolored ribbon and jaunty tag add to the merriment. The snowman box and party-favor bag are decked with snowflakes and a frosty snowman on foam mounting tape who'll pop right off the surface! The decorations are minimal, the spirits high, the feeling magical!

♥

THREE BOXES OF VARYING SIZES OR COLORS PROVIDE THE BASE FOR A GREAT THEMED CELEBRATION.

♥

VELLUM FAVORITES

Delicate, translucent vellum, a favorite paper of paper crafters, is an extraordinary material. We love overlapping parts of vellum images to create texture and to expand the palette. For this series we overlapped pastel vellum hearts, in a pleasing arrangement across the surface of a ready-made cylinder, two boxes, and a large heart layered on a greeting card. Starting with the dark colors first helps to create a base. We traced our heart sticker for this pattern.

For the heart-shaped tag attached to the cylinder, cut two contrasting colors of hearts in half and line up the cut edges on white cardstock to create a complete heart. For the other heart-shaped tags, place one vellum heart on white cardstock to create the base. Trim around the edges of the hearts with decorative scissors. Place a smaller heart of another color in the center and embellish with a crystal gem. Punch a hole at the top of the tag and tie to the box or cylinder with metallic thread or ribbon.

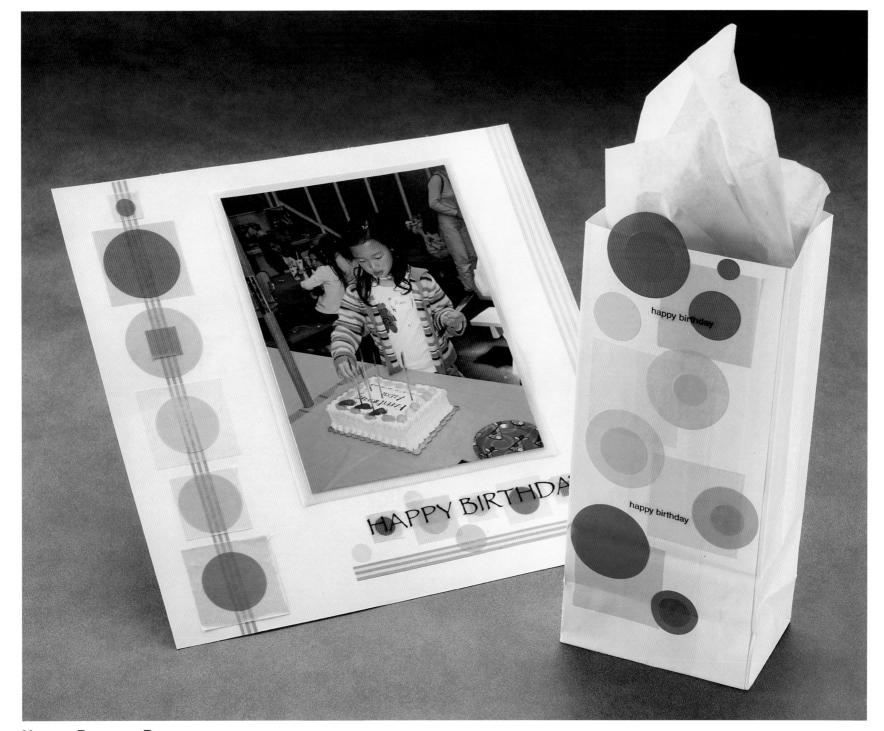

VELLUM BIRTHDAY BUBBLES

Vellum bubbles and blocks, layered and unlayered, are accompanied by vellum stripe Design Lines. The simple geometric shapes march down the side of the album page, and float dreamily across the surface and off the top edge of a party bag. A decorated birthday message panel supports the bottom edge of the album page while tiny birthday caption stickers complete the picture on the bag.

BIRTHDAY PARTY PANEL

Light up the room with this delightful greeting. Birthday candles adorn the bright-colored letters, supporting every upright, even bending to support some! We composed the decorated letters on sticker liner paper before transferring them over to cardstock.

Fold yellow cardstock to create a 3 5/8 x 8 1/2-inch card. While stickers are still on the liner paper, cut and place candles on to vertical sections of vellum alphabet letters. Place a few of the alphabet letters on vellum panels, as shown. To center the words on the panel properly, start with the "TH" of the word "BIRTHDAY," placing the layered letters on a 3 1/8 x 8-inch white cardstock, working out to each end. Attach the white cardstock panel to the front of the card.

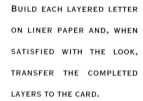

BUILD EACH LAYERED LETTER ON LINER PAPER AND, WHEN SATISFIED WITH THE LOOK, TRANSFER THE COMPLETED LAYERS TO THE CARD.

VELLUM BALLOONS

Cover the left half of a yellow card with blue paper. Add a white banner diagonally across the front of the card. Using the multi-toned blue vellum alphabet, spell out "congrats" on the banner. Add vellum balloons allowing a few to float off the top of the card to create motion. Add sparkle stars. Turn a circus lion into a graduate with a cap and diploma stickers and sit him on the top of the banner.

17

STICKER "STAMPS"

Black is a stunning canvas—this time for bright basic-color panels and stamps. This cheery design uses repetition effectively: the square color panels are repeated in a smaller size and in alternately matched basic colors. The images themselves are repetitive—stamps and hearts, and stamps with hearts. The shapes are basic, and the centered composition classic.

1. Fold a 4 $^1/_2$ high by 12 $^1/_2$-inch piece of black cardstock in half to create a 6 $^1/_4$-inch long album cover.

2. Place 1 $^1/_2$-inch square vellum blocks in each quadrant of a 3-inch square of white cardstock, leaving a narrow white margin around the edges of each block. Attach the panel to the album cover using small pieces of foam mounting tape.

3. Place 1-inch square vellum blocks in each quadrant of a 2 $^1/_4$-inch square of white paper, leaving a narrow white margin around the edges of each block. Attach this panel on top of the 3-inch cardstock panel with additional pieces of foam mounting tape.

4. Pop stickers in each quadrant of the 2 $^1/_4$-inch square, carefully aligning the stickers to inside margins to keep design evenly balanced.

5. Punch small holes at each end of a $^3/_4$ x 3-inch white cardstock panel. Tile $^1/_2$-inch sticky vellum blocks and small heart stickers down the length of the paper, leaving a narrow white margin around the outside edge of each block.

6. Tie paper panel to the left edge of album cover, tucking the ends of $^1/_8$-inch ribbon behind the end sheets on the inside covers.

THE ANTS' PICNIC

Where would we be without a sense of humor, without a sense of fun? This sticker artist has a lot of fun! One almost wants ants to come to one's next picnic to see if they really are as athletic and organized as these little fellows. Center a 1 $^3/_8$-inch yellow vellum block on a 1 $^5/_8$-inch square of white card stock. Balance a watermelon sticker on top of an ant sticker and center on a vellum panel. Attach the layered panel to the front of card by popping with foam tape. Layer food and ant stickers to create a sticker parade across the envelope flap.

SAVE LEFTOVER STICKERS, AND EVEN LEFTOVER PIECES OF STICKERS. WHO KNOWS WHAT IDEAS THEY WILL GENERATE?

POPPED HEARTS

Once again, we see black as such a dramatically supportive background color. It presents the featured attraction with great style. Here we have another use of effective repetition: bright patterned hearts against small patterned blocks. These bright-colored tiles and hearts popped with small pieces of mounting tape leap off the surface. Small patterned blocks draw our focus to the hearts. Although we used fabric block stickers for the squares on these projects, interesting printed papers would work just as well. The box has an unusual top. Is the heart emerging from the box or diving into it?

FOR THE BOX:
1. Create the box out of black cardstock using an Ellison slant-top box die-cut.
2. Place 1-inch bright fabric block stickers or printed patterned papers in a centered column on each panel of the box.
3. Pop fabric hearts on top of each fabric or printed paper block.
4. Create a red polka dot heart (we traced our red heart sticker), add the greeting panel across the width of the heart.
5. Tuck the heart with greeting in the slot on top of the box.

FOR THE CARD:
1. Tile a row of five 1-inch fabric block stickers or printed patterned paper across the front of the card.
2. Pop fabric hearts on top of each block.
3. Create fabric greeting panel and center horizontally below the tiled panel of hearts.

19

LAYERED BABY FRAME

An ensemble of charming projects containing a baby announcement, frame, and thank-you card is decorated in a palette of soft yellow and complementary baby colors. The yellow background creates a warm stage to display the joyful images. The soft, engaging palette is appealing, especially against the varying textures of the cardstock and the variety in the cut edges of the panels. Notice the many popped layers, which add dimension. The dimensions need not be exact. Cut successively larger openings in the frames to create textured, layered mats around the photographs. There are a lot of cutting steps for this frame, but it is not difficult.

1. Wrap a 6 x 6-inch frame with a green stripe fabric sticker sheet.
2. Cut a 5^3/$_8$-inch ruffle-edge yellow paper frame using an Ellison Wiggle die-cut.
3. Cut a 3 ^{3}/$_4$-inch yellow paper square and cut a 3 ^{1}/$_4$-inch square out of the center.
4. Cut a 3 ^{3}/$_4$-inch blue paper square and cut a 2 ^{15}/$_{16}$-inch square out of the center.
5. Layer paper squares to create mats: blue on the bottom, followed by the ruffle-edge yellow, and then, the yellow square on top.
6. Attach layered paper panels to photo frame using small pieces of mounting tape.
7. Build a small sticker arrangement with fabric shapes and caption, and attach to lower right corner of the yellow ruffle frame with small pieces of mounting tape.
8. Add photo, and center a pink bow sticker above the photo.

BIRTH ANNOUNCEMENT

1. Place a 2 ^{7}/$_8$ x 3 ^{3}/$_4$-inch stripe fabric panel on top of a 2^1/$_8$ x 4-inch pale yellow cardstock panel. Trim the outside edge of the yellow panel with decorative scissors.
2. Decorate the fabric panel with a blue oval tag and add a row of baby motif stickers, popping each off the surface with a small piece of foam mounting tape behind each one.
3. Layer the yellow caption panel on a ^{9}/$_{16}$ x 4-inch panel of white cardstock.
4. Center two blue cardstock panels on the front of the yellow card as shown: one 2 ^{5}/$_8$ x 4 ^{1}/$_4$-inch (to hold the main image) and one ^{7}/$_8$ x 4 ^{1}/$_4$-inch (to hold the text panel).
5. Attach the mounted panels in the appropriate spots to blue cardstock, as shown, using small pieces of foam tape to add dimension.
6. Center a pink bow sticker atop the blue cardstock and overlap ribbon ends onto fabric panel.

THANK-YOU CARD

1. Mount a 1 ^{3}/$_4$ x 2 ^{1}/$_2$-inch piece of stripe fabric sticker on a 2 x 2 ^{3}/$_4$-inch panel of yellow textured cardstock and trim the outside edges with decorative scissors.
2. Decorate a blue square panel with baby lamb and greeting stickers popped with small pieces of foam mounting tape. Place the decorated panel on the stripe panel, and add the heart sticker partially off the top of the blue square, as shown.
3. Center a 2 ^{1}/$_4$ x 3-inch piece of blue cardstock on a 3 ^{1}/$_4$ x 5-inch yellow textured notecard.
4. Attach the layered stripe panel on top, using small pieces of foam mounting tape.

ADD DIMENSION TO PAPER CRAFTS BY PLACING SMALL PIECES OF FOAM MOUNTING TAPE BEHIND PAPER PANELS OR STICKERS. YOU WILL NEED TO APPLY A DAB OF BABY POWDER OR CORNSTARCH TO ANY EXPOSED ADHESIVE ON THE STICKERS TO KEEP THE ARTWORK FROM ADHERING TO INAPPROPRIATE PLACES.

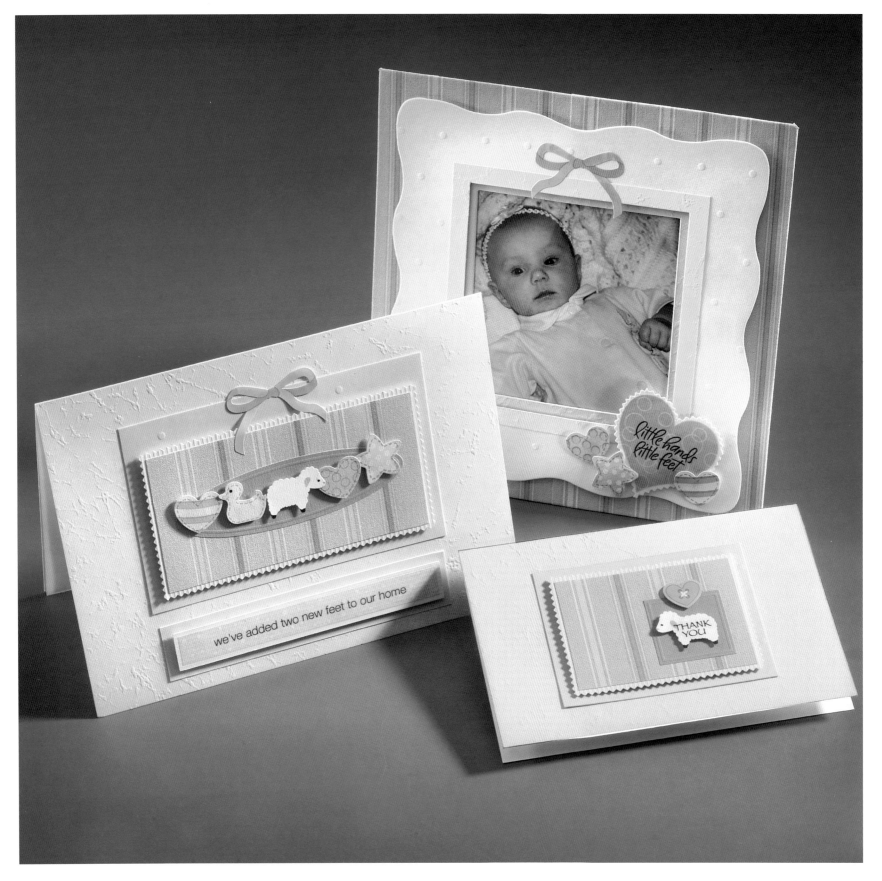

we've added two new feet to our home

little hands little feet

THANK YOU

Recipe books preserve your treasured family recipes.

Fruit Smoothie
1/2 cup non-fat yogurt
1/2 cup milk
1/2 cup frozen strawberries
1 medium bananna
1/2 cup fresh pineapple
1/4 cup orange juice

Place all the ingredients in a blender and process until smooth.

RECIPE BOOK

The Christmas cookie decorations on the cookie sheet cover of this little booklet tells everyone what is inside. A fine activity for Grandmother and grandchild on a mid-winter's afternoon.

1. Stack and layer white album pages between two sheets of yellow cardstock cut to size, creating the recipe album. Score covers and pages $^3/_4$ inch from left-hand edge.

2. Place two metal nail head stickers $1^1/_2$ inches apart on left side of cover and punch a small hole through each center. Insert album pages between the covers and repunch through the holes and album pages. Bind together with red string.

3. Cut a rectangle from a metallic sticker sheet; and fold the left edge in $^1/_4$ inch to create the cookie sheet lip. Attach to white cardstock trimmed to same size, and angle on textured red cardstock, slipping a mitt sticker behind lower right corner of the sheet. Pop cookie stickers across the cookie sheet, and add the title. Frame the cardstock edge with narrow blue Design Lines

4. Decorate recipe cards with additional stickers.

RECIPE PORTFOLIO

A sturdy little recipe booklet containing favorite child-friendly recipes inspires us to involve our children in many of our daily activities. Children usually love to cook. Keep the recipe collection in a safe place and add to it as you cook and create new recipes with your children.

1. Fold textured red cardstock to create a 6 x 6 ³/₄-inch portfolio.

2. Layer a complementary color panel, and a decorated type panel on the front cover.

3. Wrap a 3 x 6 ³/₄-inch panel of fabric or printed paper around the bottom edge of the portfolio, so it extends 1 ¹/₂ inches up on the front cover and inside cover.

4. Cut bear stickers in half while they are still on the liner paper.

5. Place large bear (top half only) on album cover, lining cut bear edge with top edge of fabric sheet.

6. Tuck small bears on top of large bear, again aligning cut edges with top edge of fabric.

7. Add chef's hat and utensil.

8. Using template on page 125, create a pocket from white cardstock covered with a fabric full sheet for the inside back cover of the portfolio.

9. Embellish the pocket with bear stickers and border the outside edges of the inside back cover with red patterned Design Lines.

10. Print recipe cards on computer, or write them out yourself, and embellish with sticker art and Design Line borders. Tuck recipe cards inside portfolio pocket.

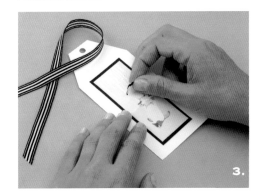

REFLECTION TIME

Mirror-image stickers make it possible to have two characters face one another, or create a reflection in a pond or on ice. Just remember that the reflecting surface should be one that naturally reflects: a mirror, water, or ice. This tag can be used as a gift tag or a bookmark, or it can embellish a card or scrapbook page.

1. Cut a light blue tag, about 6 x 2 ³/₄ inches. Layer a piece of black cardstock, 1 ³/₄ x 4 inches, on top. Layer a piece of light blue cardstock 1 ¹/₂ x 3 ³/₄ inches on top of the black one. Add a piece of icicle Design Line to the top of the blue cardstock. Select two matching penguins that face in opposite directions. Attach one upside down, below an imaginary horizon line.

2. Tear a piece of light blue vellum to fit over this penguin and align with the edges of the blue cardstock panel. (The torn edge resembles a shoreline, and establishes the horizon line.)

3. Place the second penguin above the shoreline, aligning the feet with the first penguin. Punch a hole and add a black and white ribbon to the tag.

FLAMINGO REFLECTION

1. Fold a 3 ⁷/₈ x 13 ¹/₂-inch panel of textured paper to create a 3 ⁷/₈ x 6 ³/₄-inch card.

2. Cut a 2 ³/₄ x 5-inch panel from blue cardstock. Draw two light pencil guide lines across the panel ¹/₈ inch apart.

3. Align bottom edges of grass stickers and feet of the flamingo stickers on the outside edges of the lines. Gently erase any remaining pencil lines.

4. Tear the top edge of a 2 ³/₄-inch square of pale blue vellum and place on top of the lower portion of the sticker picture, aligning the top edge with the bottom of the flamingo's feet.

5. Place the panel on top of layered vellum paper rectangles and attach to card.

GLACIER PENGUIN REFLECTION

1. Cut two identical blue glacier shapes from blue vellum. Trim the second glacier down so it is ten percent smaller than the original size.

2. Lightly trace a pencil line across the center of paper. Attach the glacier shapes on either side of the line, the smaller one on the bottom.

3. Place penguin stickers on either side of the line, aligning feet at the line. Gently erase remaining pencil marks.

4. Attach 3 $^1/_4$ x 6 $^3/_4$-inch blue vellum panel across the bottom half of the page to cover lower glacier shape.

5. Finish artwork with a sprinkle of snowball stickers, or add the snow dots with a white pen.

BLUE VELLUM POND REFLECTION

1. Fold a 3 $^3/_4$ x 18-inch panel of textured cardstock to create a 3 $^3/_4$ x 9-inch card.

2. Center a 2 $^3/_4$ x 7 $^1/_8$-inch blue cardstock panel on a slightly larger panel of black paper. Create a deckle edge by cutting the black paper with decorative scissors.

3. Lightly trace a pencil line across the center of the blue panel. Carefully position some cattail stickers above and below the line. Add butterfly stickers above and below the line. Gently erase remaining pencil marks.

4. Tear the top edge of a 3 $^3/_4$ x 2 $^3/_4$-inch panel of blue vellum and attach to cover the bottom half of the sticker image.

5. Layer small section of water vellum Design Line just beneath torn paper edge.

6. Complete picture by adding water circle stickers to top surface of blue vellum.

7. Attach layered paper panel to front of card.

WINTER CARDS

Asoft, pleasing palette supports the soft, raised vellum panels in this trio of winter cards. By varying the specific winter image you feature, you can create your Christmas cards quickly, and still individualize each one. These soft wintry cards are favorites of ours. They can be Christmas or New Year's cards, or seasonal note cards.

1. For each card cut three squares of light blue vellum (3 inches, 2 ³/₈ inches, and 2 inches) and layer on matching cards.

2. Add one of a variety of frosty winter stickers.

3. Sprinkle tiny snowflakes on each card, placing some on the larger pieces of vellum for a see-through look.

HARVEST MENU

Sage, yellow, and gold mats support the colorful glory of these natural autumnal harvest stickers. The design is easy: the shape of the sticker almost tells you to feature it centerstage. Here it is at the center top of a menu card or centered in the foreground on the place card. With a consistent palette, the results are stunning.

1. Print your menu centered on white paper. Trim down to a 5 1/4-inch square.
2. Layer a square of sage textured cardstock (6 ³/₄ inches) with a 6 ¹/₂-inch square of yellow cardstock and add the printed menu panel.
3. Frame the outside edge of the menu panel with narrow metallic Design Line stickers.
4. Pop a harvest sticker at the center top of the menu panel with small pieces of foam tape.

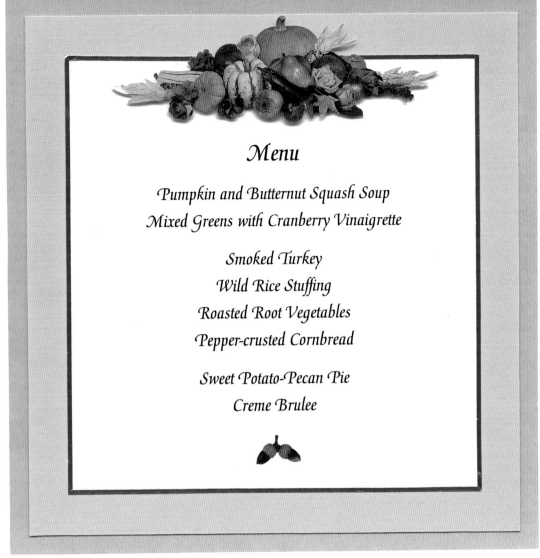

Menu

Pumpkin and Butternut Squash Soup
Mixed Greens with Cranberry Vinaigrette

Smoked Turkey
Wild Rice Stuffing
Roasted Root Vegetables
Pepper-crusted Cornbread

Sweet Potato-Pecan Pie
Creme Brulee

HARVEST PLACE CARD

1. Fold sage cardstock to create 2 ¹/₂ x 3-inch place card.
2. Center 1 ¹/₂ x 3-inch panel of yellow paper on front of card.
3. Border top edge of yellow paper and bottom edge of place card with narrow metallic Design Line stickers.
4. Pop harvest sticker along bottom edge of yellow paper with small pieces of foam tape.

THREE BOXES

Centered, layered medallions speak of stable and structured classic design with symmetrical balance. These three containers are elegant reminders of well-balanced elements. The idea is clean: center one sticker on another one or two, and center the medallion on the cylinder or box.

LAYERED VELLUM POPPIES (FACING PAGE)

In the card on the left, two soft-yellow poppy blossoms are cut. One is layered onto a Mulberry paper-wrapped mat between two perfect green leaves. The second poppy is slightly crinkled and then popped on top of the first one. The crinkled edges of the top blossom add detail and dimension to the card. The card on the right offers one poppy on a narrow panel that is layered and popped off the surface, leaving the poppy edges to drape loosely to the panel underneath. Two dimensional effects created by layering and popping.

METALLIC SHAPES

Strong colors—copper, gold, and black—are offered in a confident, dramatic design. The strong basic shapes—squares, star, heart—are lifted from a stark platform with foam mounting tape. The symmetrical composition is shifted off-center, adding to a sense of motion. The torn edges of the paper soften the effect.

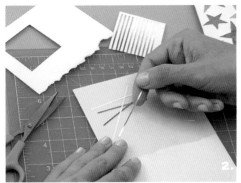

METALLIC STARS CARD

Soft, undulating torn edges of cardstock and vellum provide a gentle shoreline image complete with a break-away star sprinkled with drops of magical dust. The window above adds intrigue with bits of streamers, gold dust, and metallic stars, but from where? One can tell magical stories with sticker art.

1. Fold pink textured cardstock to create a 4 $\frac{1}{2}$ x 6 $\frac{1}{4}$-inch card. Punch or die-cut a small square window in the upper left corner of soft pink cardstock. Tear the edge of cardstock about $\frac{3}{4}$–inch below the window. Tear the edge of a sheet of pink vellum. Attach torn vellum to the front of the card, aligning at the top.

2. Cut small strips of metallic and solid pastel Design Line stickers and create a design on the pink vellum so it will be seen on the card, inside the die-cut window.

3. Layer the windowed cardstock on the decorated pink vellum. Decorate the torn edges of the papers with tiny confetti pieces cut from metallic Design Line stickers.

4. Attach additional Design Line sections to the surface of a metallic star. Pop metallic stars in die-cut window and on the torn edge of vellum paper.

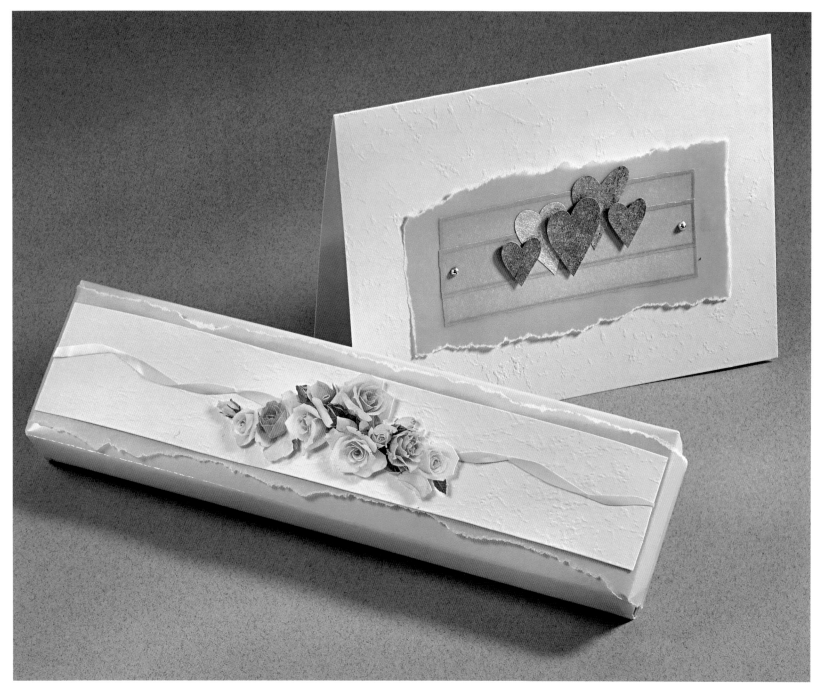

TORN, LAYERED VELLUM

Elegant, textured cardstock, torn vellum, a layered vellum panel, and a mesmerizing layered arrangement of popped metallic hearts offers a sophisticated card that would be hard to give up. Two stickers plus sumptuous layered cardstock and torn vellum make an exquisite gift wrap for a very special gift. The long, lean line of the box itself is echoed in the long, lean composition, and the choice of long, lean stickers. The undulating torn edges of the vellum complement the straight lines of the card and box.

VELLUM TEARS VERY EASILY. HOLD IT FIRMLY ENOUGH, BUT NOT TIGHT, AND PULL GENTLY TOWARD OR AWAY FROM YOU.

*Bright colors
are infectious;
they can lift
our spirits
and provoke
a smile.*

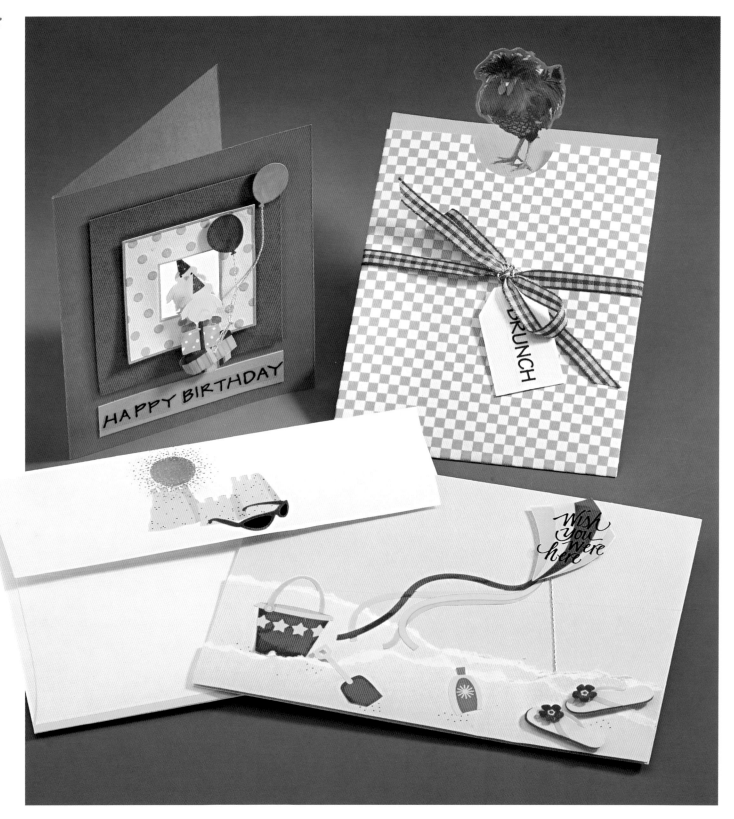

CHICK REFLECTION

You don't often have a front and back view of an image. This little chick begged to be seen from all sides. And there he is surprising himself in the mirror (just like every toddler we know). The colors shout joy and celebration, and this little fellow is full of it. Here we "popped" the balloons and the chick on the pile of presents by placing small pieces of mounting tape on the back of the images.

1. Layer a 3-inch red square on a purple 4 x 4 $^1/_2$-inch card leaving equal space on the top and both sides, and extra room beneath for the type panel.
2. Mount a square of shiny metal ("mirror") paper behind a beige polka-dot frame with blue edges and layer the frame on the red square.
3. Select two little chicks, one facing forward and one facing away, and cut tiny hats for each from red cardstock. Put the front-facing chick in the mirror, trimming as necessary.
4. Pile up a few tiny presents, and add the other chick at the top. Pop the gifts and chick onto the card.
5. Add fine silver cord behind small balloons; add mounting tape and pop the balloons on the card, tucking the strings under the chick's foot.
6. Add the type panel below the picture.

BRUNCH INVITATION

Try creating a folded pocket envelope with bright-colored printed paper for a special invitation. This is one of our favorite techniques. It's simple, effective, and fun. We literally wrapped the flat card with printed paper to create a pocket for it, gluing the pocket together at the back. For an expert finish, cut edges of the bottom flap on the diagonal. Decorate the pocket and the card as you wish. We couldn't resist the Extraordinary Chicken for a brunch invitation.

BEACH DAY

With a few snips here and there we tailored the stickers to fit their spots on the beach. Decorating the envelope gives a preview of coming attractions to the recipient and a smile to the mailman!

1. Tear two strips of sandy beige paper and layer on yellow card, to create sand.
2. Use a silver design line or real string, for the kite string. Pop the kite on the string and add the "Wish you were here" caption.
3. Tuck the bucket between the layers of sand and add the flip flops plus flowers. Cut the edge of the shovel and bottle so they appear to be stuck into the sand.
4. Adding a few groups of dots with a fine point black pen will make the sand look more realistic.
5. Add a reflection sun and a few extra stickers to your envelope.

IF YOU TEAR PAPERS THAT ARE COLORED ON ONE SIDE AND WHITE ON THE OTHER, YOU WILL SEE THE WHITE ON THE TORN EDGE. THIS IS A GREAT WAY TO CREATE THE EFFECT OF SAND, SNOW, OR FROTH ON WAVES OR ICE CREAM.

LAVENDER FLOWER POT

Most of Mrs. Grossman's stickers are printed as mirror images (identical shapes facing in opposite directions). Sometimes two stickers are needed. Back stickers with their mirror images if you want to have some of your sticker art off the page and would like it to be viewed from two sides. It does wonders, adding weight to support the portion off the edge, and a finished view from both front and back.

1. Cut a sheet of metallic paper to 4 x 6 inches. Cover the metallic sheet with orchid card stock. Using the template on page 125, cut out the pot pattern from the orchid paper-backed metallic sheet, and fold. Cut out 2 "Inside Liner" shapes from the same template.

2. Cut out two pot rims, one from the metallic sheet and one from grey vellum. Leaving the backer on the sticker, trim the bottom edge of pot rim with decorative-edged scissors. Trim the bottom of the vellum pot rim with the same scalloped scissors. Remove the backer from the metallic rim and carefully place the rim onto the vellum rim, leaving about $1/8$ inch of the vellum showing at the bottom. Trim the extra $1/8$-inch off the top of the metallic rim. Add mounting tape to the back of the layered rims, and pop the rim onto the pot.

3. Peel lavender sticker off its backer and powder the back with baby powder (to remove the adhesive). Place the powdered sticker down on a piece of dark paper (to see the edges more clearly when working on the stickers) with the powdered back side up.

4. Peel second lavender sticker off its backer and carefully place it back-to-back with the first lavender sticker. Repeat these two steps three times. (There are three sets of back-to-back stickers on this card.)

5. Tape one back-to-back lavender sticker centered on the inside of the front of the card, and two back-to-back lavender stickers on the inside of the back of the card. Attach the white liners over the taped lavender stickers on both sides of the inside of the card. The liners cover the tape and provide a writing surface.

Variations on a Theme

These charming pots of flowers are made the same way as the galvanized metal pot of lavender. Color changes the effect, but not the process or techniques.

FOR GREEN FLOWER POT WITH DAISIES:

1. Use template to create green paper flower pot. Select a lighter shade for the top edge.
2. Wrap fabric Design Line across top edge, folding and powdering ends to create bow.
3. Add back-to-back daisies, trimming and cutting bouquet to fit inside card liner.

FOR RED FLOWER POT WITH HEARTS:

1. Reduce template to create a smaller red flower pot, using striped paper for top edge.
2. Wrap a 1/4-inch wide satin ribbon across top edge to create bow.
3. Add back-to-back hearts and vine stickers to create flowers, tucking sticker stems inside card liner.

FOR RED AND WHITE TULIP CARD:

1. Create pot using template.
2. Arrange tulips on white card and add pot made with sage green textured cardstock and vellum, and add pink bow. Mount on sage green textured card.

WHEN USING STICKERS BACK TO BACK, REMEMBER TO CAREFULLY LINE UP THE TWO STICKER SHAPES, AND ATTACH THEM STICKY SIDE TO STICKY SIDE. LEAVE THE STICKERS ON THE LINER PAPER WHEN CUTTING; REMOVE IT WHEN YOU ARE READY TO PLACE THE STICKER ON YOUR ARTWORK.

BUILDING BOUQUETS

Building a bouquet of flowers is a wonderful challenge. Cut and layer individual flower stickers until you have created your ideal arrangement. This group is quite simple.

1. Build a flower bouquet on front of a sage green card.

2. Diecut two Sizzix buckets, one from a full sheet of silver metallic paper, and the other from copper.

3. Build the bucket on the card in layers, placing the bucket base down first, making sure that the top edge covers the flower stems.

4. Silhouette the copper handle and attach it over the silver one. Attach the bucket rim and layered handle components to the card using small pieces of foam tape to add dimension.

5. Pop a few more flower blossoms on top of the original bouquet to add depth and dimension.

FORMAL BOUQUET

Soft colors, long stems, and a long, pale satin ribbon all contribute to a slightly formal floral presentation. The loose arrangement is almost unexpected, and appealing, like a just-gathered armful of favorite blossoms for an old-fashioned friend. The centered arrangement and the soft, pleasing palette of both the flowers themselves and the cardstock extend the gracious sensibility.

WHEN POPPING STICKERS IN A BOUQUET, DON'T FORGET TO POWDER THE EXPOSED BACK OF EACH STICKER BEFORE YOU ATTACH IT TO THE PROJECT SURFACE! A LIGHT DUSTING OF POWDER MAKES SURE YOUR STICKER ART STAYS "POPPED" UP OFF THE PAGE. LEAVE LINER PAPER OR FOAM TAPE IN PLACE WHILE POWDERING SO YOU CAN ATTACH THE STICKER TO ANY VARIETY OF SURFACES.

♥

WRAPPED BOUQUET

A newspaper-wrapped bouquet of flowers is such a romantic image: a spur-of-the-moment expression of love. Everyone who saw this card instantly smiled. The scene is created with cut, layered, and popped flowers, that are then wrapped in newspaper and tied with a little piece of string, and then glued to a card. This one has to come from your heart. The directions are to create a bouquet as you like it, remembering negative space, and remembering the power of lifting the blooms off the surface of the card—popping them. The simple black and white newspaper ties together any palette. The string could be any color, but this orange echoes a few of the blooms in the bouquet.

POPPED BOUQUET

The stems of a bright and cheerful small bouquet of tulips, narcissus, and freesia are tied with a yellow ribbon. The mix should be your own, naturally depending on the stickers you have. The slight angle of the flowers on the page lends a casual, informal air. The layered mats combine to support the central image, as well as the palette.

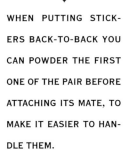

WHEN PUTTING STICK-
ERS BACK-TO-BACK YOU
CAN POWDER THE FIRST
ONE OF THE PAIR BEFORE
ATTACHING ITS MATE, TO
MAKE IT EASIER TO HAN-
DLE THEM.

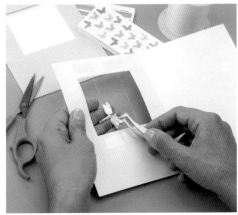

DRAGONFLY CARD

Dragonflies and butterflies flying against green hills in the distance are seen through a framed window. The pearly colors of these fabulous iridescent dragonfly and butterfly stickers change subtly as they flutter and the lighting shifts. Here they are back-to-back on a monofilament hung vertically.

1. Cut two die-cut window cards from sage green textured cardstock. Cut one window card in half down the length of the fold, and set aside. Frame the window on the front of the second card with vellum Design Line stickers.

2. Cut two pieces of monofilament slightly longer than the window. Tape them at the top and bottom of the window on the inside of the card. Add dragonflies and butterflies to the filament one by one, carefully turning card over and back-to-back each one.

3. Glue the half of the card that you reserved in step 1 onto the inside of the card front, covering the taped ends of the monofilament. Create hills by tearing two vellum squares in opposite directions, layer over each other, and glue. Layer this to a sage textured-cardstock square directly behind the window on the inside, right-hand side of the card.

FOUR-FOLD CHRISTMAS CARD

A colorful, four-compartment, windowed Christmas card with hanging back-to-back wrapped gifts dangling on monofilament in front of our eyes is sure to delight. The ornamented popped and layered panels in each compartment sing the message for all to hear. The sculptural card stands on its star frame, ready to deck the halls for a festive holiday season.

CIRCUS TRAIN

A delightful series of projects created for a young-ster's birthday-party table includes a circus train car for the table decoration, two place cards, and two party-favor bags, all continuing the theme established with the invitation. The palette is young and festive. The balloons, animals, circus-car tires, and the wavy trim are all stickers. Don't stop here; use your imagina-tion, and expand the collection.

The train car looks a bit daunting, but with the template, it is not difficult. The cut and fold lines are well marked, and once you start you will see the car emerge quickly. Probably the most intricate step is folding the giraffe's and elephant's feet out so they stand on them splayed out as a base. Use heavy cardstock if you want the train car to be sturdy enough to sit on the table.

1. Enlarge the template for the circus train car on page 126 as necessary and affix to red cardstock with temporary adhesive. With a craft knife and a sturdy ruler (on a cutting surface) cut out train car. Cut solid lines, score dashed lines.

2. Fold at score lines. With double-sided tape or glue, assemble train car.

3. Fold a small piece of liner paper in half, with the slick side out. Back-to-back the giraffe sticker, placing the folded liner paper between it's feet. Do the same for the elephant.

4. Back-to-back balloons on wire. Add vellum panel to the back of the elephant to create a blanket. Trim off excess vellum panel. Place monkey on elephant's back, anchoring the feet. Powder back of monkey. Twist the three balloons together on wire. Place the wire in the monkey's hand. Tape wire to the back of elephant.

5. Place slate mulberry paper (papier) circle centered on each cut-out wheel. Cut the center from the tire and place it centered on the mulberry paper circle. Punch hole in center of wheel using a $1/16$-inch hole punch. Place red and blue vellum design line sticker across the top front of train car. Trim off excess. Using small white brads, attach wheels to train car.

6. Fold out the giraffe's feet and affix them to the inside of train car. Poke the giraffe's head through the "bars" on the top of the train car. Repeat the above with the elephant, poking the balloons through the "bars" on the top of the train car.

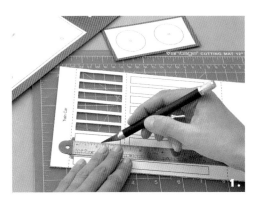

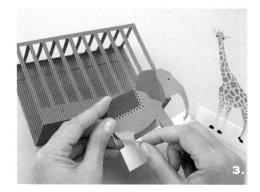

MATS, FRAMES, BORDERS, & WINDOWS

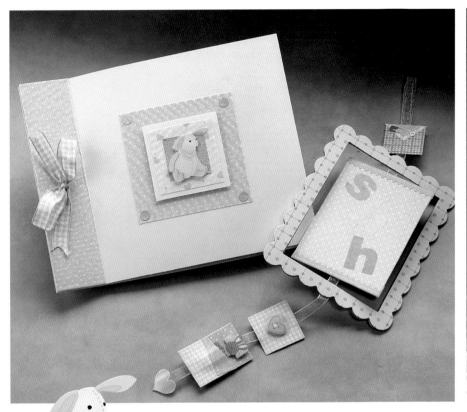

There are supporting roles for sticker art projects, just as there are for stage and film productions. Mats, frames, borders, and windows are the supporting roles for the featured players in the sticker art world. Mats support by presenting the starring image. Frames do just that: they frame the stars. Borders define the space for the stars, and windows give us a special peek inside to see the magic.

In this chapter we have included projects that range from very simple stationery with matted and unmatted sticker images to full-scale constructed scenes with perspective and even a proscenium.

Mrs. Grossman's Paper Company makes stickers in all shapes and sizes. Some of the most supportive concepts are the fabulous sticker paper sheets—everything from fabric to metallic to glorious textured sheets. You can cut mats in any shape or size from these beautiful sheet stickers and adhere them to your work, or you can cut mats from your own paper and glue them down to your card or paper, or you can use panel stickers. However you do it, you are creating the

set, or the scene, for the stars. Working with stickers is exciting and so much fun when you think of the process as building a set or a scene. We find that keeping such an image in mind inspires creativity and confidence. It helps you direct your attention to the focal point of your art. All of these elements—mats, frames, borders, and windows—help define the space, and balance the positive and negative space that is so crucial to successful sticker art.

Paper arts are fabulous. You can combine textures, colors, and shapes in a variety of ways. Think about all three elements when composing a project. We have combined textured paper with smooth cardstock or vellum, fabric stickers with metallic stickers or textured cardstock, or smooth vellum in varying colors. Experiment yourself. And have fun.

Turn a simple sticker into a beautiful well-composed presentation with well-coordinated mats and frames. Layering mats of contrasting or coordinating colors and textures adds depth and focus.

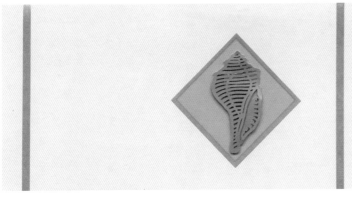

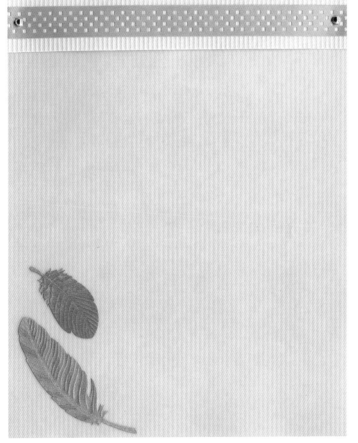

STATIONERY

Creating your own distinctive stationery with Mrs. Grossman's stickers is a pleasure. And the results are stunning. Not compelled to live with several hundred sheets of a printed design, you are free to create one-of-a-kind, or as many of each as you wish. We love to make sets of these as gifts for any number of occasions, for any degree of formality or informality, and for any age. When creating your own stationery, remember that a tasteful decorative element is just perfect. Choose and stay with a pleasing palette. The cool pastel tones with neutral accents are just right.

A shell, a square, two vertical lines. These sheets are easy and fun to create. A simple image layered and placed at an interesting angle creates a clean, elegant look. The muted colors complete the feeling of serenity.

Five blocks of three textured layers of successively larger metallic vellum squares run along the base of a soft blue note card. Tiny squares, punctuated with tiny gems, stand sentinel on either end of the row of squares. The center layered square has a matching tiny gem, completing the balance.

Two feathers adorn the lower left corner of a lavender page. The top of the stationery folds over about 1/2 inch and is embellished with a laser-cut Design Line border. Tiny gems anchor each end of the border.

ENVELOPES DO NOT HAVE TO BE EXACT REPLICAS OF THE STATIONERY. TRY PICKING UP ONE OF THE SECONDARY COLORS.

IVORY CARD WITH BLOSSOM FLOURISH

We used a 5 x 7-inch ivory card and envelope and added elegant metallic vellum stickers to give it a personal touch. The beautiful flower flourish is laser cut for delicacy.

IVORY STATIONERY WITH GINKGO LEAVES

We used ivory paper bordered in gold, and added just one gold vellum ginkgo leaf. For the envelope, place two gold vellum Design Lines cut at an angle over the flap and add a silver ginkgo for accent.

BLUE AND GRAY STATIONERY

We started with a sheet of blue stationery, attached a piece of dark gray vellum torn to fit on the top, and added a laser-cut medallion off-center over the torn vellum line. A tiny vellum panel in the center of the medallion holds a blue stone accent.

BASEBALL ALBUM

Sticker art is for everyone, all ages, all interests. Can you think of an imaginative use for an old torn leather shoelace? How about as the binding for a baseball album for a young baseball fan? We've included the shoelace piece with textured cardstock, borders, and featured a baseball sticker centerstage.

1. Fold in half a 4 x 12-inch sheet of textured black cardstock to create a 4 x 6-inch album cover.

2. Score covers 1 $^1/_4$-inches from left edge and attach a 1 $^1/_4$ x 4-inch panel of textured red cardstock on outside edge of cover to create spine.

3. Punch two small holes two inches apart in center of red paper and thread leather shoelace through to bind album pages inside.

4. Border left and right edges of 3$^1/_8$-inch square of sand cardstock with narrow red Design Lines and attach to front of album.

5. Place a two-inch square of sage cardstock at an angle on top of sand cardstock, as shown, attaching with a small piece of foam tape.

6. Pop baseball sticker on top of sage cardstock.

7. Create title page in the album using additional panels of sage and sand cardstock. Layer stickers and papers with small pieces of foam tape to add dimension to panels. Finish each page by accenting with popped baseball stickers.

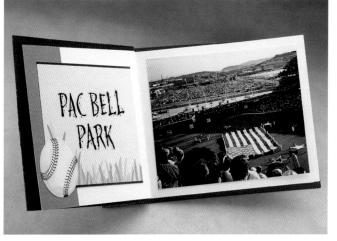

ALPHABET BLOCKS

The featured letters—A, B, C — are matted with coordinating colors, decorated, and anchored to the tops of the bright-colored, folded cubes. Use the template on page 129 for the boxes. The side panels of each block are decorated with unmatted stickers of objects beginning with each of the featured letters. A wonderful present and learning tool to make with your youngsters.

47

TAGS AND VALENTINES

There is no reason to make every tag exactly the same when you can make a set of coordinated gift tags (from one sticker sheet!). Prepare your work space with all the materials you'll need, and when you sit down to work, you'll be able to produce a set of tags, or invitations, or thank-you notes quickly.

For the Christmas tags, opposite, we simply layered red, green and white card stocks, adjusting the sizes and color to fit the stickers. Each Christmas cookie is "popped" with foam tape. Punch a tiny hole and add contrasting red or green ribbon.

For the Valentines, below, we used pink or lime green mats on small red cards to show off our frog prince and love bugs. The energetic colors send a delightful carefree message to that special someone. These little valentines are sure to be noticed.

WE MADE THE SET OF NINE GIFT TAGS FROM ONE STICKER SHEET, WITH A FEW IMAGES LEFT OVER. AND WE DID IT IN JULY! DON'T WAIT UNTIL DECEMBER TO MAKE YOUR CARDS AND TAGS IF YOU DON'T HAVE TO. AS SOON AS YOU KNOW HOW YOU WANT TO DESIGN YOUR TAGS AND CARDS, DO IT.

PUP FABRIC FRAME

Wouldn't it be fun to decorate your dog's picture frame with embellishments he would like? Paw prints, a tennis ball, and another friendly pooch are just the right elements. This frame has been color-coordinated to the color of the golden retriever.

1. Cut or die-cut a $3^5/8$-inch opening in the center of a 5 $^1/4$-inch square frame, and cover with fabric sticker or printed paper.

2. Decorate frame with paw print stickers and place plush tennis ball and dog patch in lower left corner. Powder any exposed adhesive on the back of the patch overlapping into the frame opening.

3. Place the photo inside the frame opening, and attach the frame to a card or page surface.

CHICK FABRIC FRAME

This charming fabric frame is finished with an adorable plush fabric chick. The plush stickers can be glued onto artwork or even ironed on to fabric clothing—like T-shorts or overalls. They add lots of texture. You can cover a small commercial frame with fabric stickers, add Design Line borders and make a bow with a fabric Design Line sticker. The little yellow chick stands out on the pastel pink frame.

BABY ALBUM

Adorable, thoughtful baby gifts: a sweet baby album with a handmade sticker art cover and a hanging Sh-h-h sign to hang from a doorknob or to tack on the baby room doorframe while the baby is sleeping. The palette for each of these projects is pleasing and soft, combining ivory and pink, and lavender and yellow. The "sleeping baby" sign has dangling decorative panels, like a flying kite. Let your imagination take wing, and add your own decorated panels.

TRAVEL JOURNAL COVER

Aglamorous old-fashioned cover for a glamorous cruise-vacation journal. An appealing soft green background is completed with metallic trim, orchids, and vellum. And you must be meeting the group for shuffleboard on deck at 4:00 PM!

Cut, layer, and pop orchid and butterfly stickers to decorate the surface of the frame. The multi-layered mats add interest and texture.

Special photographs need special frames. Unique frames add a festive note and will make any photograph special. The meandering metallic leaves on the frame above lend an extravagant touch: a message that says there is time to meander and enjoy life. The blue fabric print below captures the joyful moment of a little boy in a garden.

METALLIC LEAVES FRAME

1. Wrap metallic full sheet around a 4 x 5-inch cardstock or cardboard photo frame with a 2 x 3$\frac{1}{2}$-inch opening.
2. Hand-cut leaves from metallic sheet and wrap around gold metallic wire.
3. Twine metal thread around surface of frame, tacking in place with tiny pieces of foam tape behind each leaf.

BLUE FABRIC FRAME

1. Wrap a 5 x 6$\frac{5}{8}$-inch piece of cardstock or cardboard with fabric sheet.
2. Wrap a 4 x 6$\frac{3}{8}$-inch piece of cardstock or cardboard with fabric sheet and mount a 3$\frac{3}{8}$ x 5$\frac{7}{8}$-inch photograph on top.
3. Pop photo frame on top of larger fabric mat, using small pieces of foam tape to attach.
4. Wrap fabric Design Line stickers kitty-corner around lower left and upper right corners of frame. Accent corner borders with button stickers.

VACATION DREAMING

A fashionable resort scene is featured behind a framed vellum window, the curve of the coastline pulling us into the picture. And the lovely flower-draped white wicker rocking chair in front of the window beckons us to sit awhile and dream. The composition, the perspective, and the palette are all coordinated.

1. Cut or die-cut a 2 ³/₄-inch square window on the card front.

2. Build beach scene inside the window, cutting and layering stickers to fit on the back panel of the card.

3. Attach a 3-inch square of pale blue vellum paper inside window. Frame outside of window with narrow Design Lines.

4. While wicker chair sticker is still on liner paper, drape the lei sticker across the chair, gently lifting portions of chair sticker off liner paper to tuck sticker in and behind it.

5. Cut trinks from palm trees and group with remaining flowers on front of card under window.

6. Carefully transfer chair sticker art from liner paper to surface of card, overlapping top of chair into lower right corner of window. Add a few more flowers to finish the arrangement.

PEGASUS BIRTHDAY CARD

Fairy dust, a pegasus, and stars float among the clouds in this multi-matted imaginative story. The palette is engaging.

1. Layer 3 x 5-inch lavender and 2 ¹/₂ x 4¹/₂-inch purple paper panels together on front of blue card.

2. Place a 1 ³/₄ x 3 ³/₄-inch bordered vellum panel on a 2 x 4-inch piece of light blue cardstock. Build sticker scene on top of vellum panel, placing sun, fairy dust, and a cloud sticker directly on the surface. Pop the pegasus and two more clouds on top of the scene.

3. Pop the blue paper panel to the front of the card.

4. Build greeting with fairy dust on the sticker liner and transfer to the lower right corner of the card.

5. Wrap silver threads around the left side of card and back-to-back star stickers on the thread ends to add a decorative closure or band.

WINDOW STARS

No doubt at all, the stars are the star of this striking card. The fireworks-decorated stars are featured, popping out of the centered window. And the card, no doubt, is meant for someone who is a star!

1. Place a 1 ¾-inch square of silver metallic ribbed cardstock about 1 ¾ inches down from the top center of black card.

2. Punch a 3-inch square from blue cardstock paper and then punch or die cut a 1 ½-inch square in its center.

3. Place a clear caption sticker on the lower right side of frame. Pop frame over silver cardstock square, attaching with foam tape.

4. Place fireworks stickers on a piece of black cardstock. Punch out stars using a star paper punch.

5. Pop stars in window on card, attaching with foam tape.

You did it!

YOU CAN EXTEND A STICKER'S USEFULNESS BY CUTTING SHAPES FROM A STICKERED SURFACE. YOU CAN PUNCH OR DIE-CUT A VARIETY OF SHAPES FROM STICKERS ADHERED TO CARDSTOCK, VELLUM, OR CLEAR FILM.

WINDOW CARDS

You may remember the fun of shaker boxes when you were young. They are just as intriguing now—perfect holiday cards or gifts. We've adapted the idea, and created three different shaker-box cards to show you. One featuring a wintertime photo of an adorable child, complete with glitter-snow. Another contains fish and coral stickers behind an acetate porthole. And the third composition is a lovely winterscape scene with glitter-snow. Nostalgic for sure, and fun to make. Sand, glitter, or micro-beads work well in the shaker boxes.

FOR THE CHILD'S PHOTO CARD:

1. Fold a $6^1/4$ x 9-inch piece of cardstock in half to create a $4^1/2$ x $6^1/4$-inch card. Cut a $3^3/4$-inch square from the same colored cardstock. Then cut a $3^1/4$-inch square from the center leaving a $1/4$-inch frame. Trim the outside and inside frame edge with thin metallic Design Lines.

2. Add foam tape to the back of the frame. Cut a $3^1/2$-inch square of clear acetate. Layer the acetate over the photo. Create a pocket for the glitter by sealing three sides of the acetate over the photo with white artist's tape. Fold tape around edges to the back of photo. Fill with about $1/2$ teaspoon of glitter and seal the open side with artist's tape. Adhere photo/pocket to the front of card. Place frame on the card over photo.

3. Pop Christmas garland and dust the back with powder. Add garland to the frame.

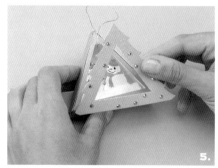

SNOWMAN ORNAMENT

To create a winter scene of snowy hills and mountains of varying heights in the windowed box, tear ivory paper strips of differing heights.

Atriangular box with snowman scene visible through the window is a Christmas tree ornament that the family can make together.

1. Cut out box pieces using template on page 126. Cut a triangle of blue vellum and attach to the inside of the box.

2. Trim the snowtree sticker to fit within the triangle; add snow and decorate background with glitter. Glue together the sides of the box. Create snowy hills by tearing two strips of ivory paper along one side. Then trim the ends of each to fit inside the box.

3. Add foam tape to the rear hill and add the snowman sticker. Powder to remove any exposed adhesive on the back of the sticker. Add foreground hill and sprinkle with glitter. Place entire snowman piece inside box and attach with foam tape.

4. Fold and tape the front of the box closed. Decorate the tree frame with gold dots, and attach to the front of the box. Tie gold string into loop and tape to top of box.

PENGUIN ORNAMENT

At your next Christmas tree-trimming party, how would you like to give each guest a handmade ornament to take home?

1. Use template on page 127 to cut out the card from light blue paper. Punch a small hole at the top. Fold on the score (dotted) line. Adhere blue paper to inside of card just below the punched hole to create the background. Trim off a small portion of a snowtree and place in the lower right corner. Tear the edge of white paper to create snow-covered ground. Attach to blue background and trim off any excess.

2. Add back view penguin to scene. Then place large snowtree (untrimmed) and icicle stickers to background using foam tape for added dimension.

3. For the front of the card, tear another piece of white paper to make snow-covered ground. Add a snowtree and penguin stickers. Powder as necessary to eliminate any exposed adhesive. Add icicles to top edge. Trim off any excess and powder as necessary. Finish card by looping ribbon through punched hole.

SIMPLE ALBUM COVERS

These handsome album covers demonstrate the influence of color on design. Each of these covers is a simple centered composition using a central image on multiple mats of varying colors. There is not much difference in the individual designs, but a substantial difference in effect. Working with harmonizing colors unleashes a flood of interesting compositions. The decorative elements are popped or simply layered central images, with additional textured papers, and a few jewel accents. Each album closes with a tied ribbon of a coordinating color.

FOLDING, COLORING, & CUTTING

There are many imaginative ways to enhance a sticker art project. Folding, coloring, and cutting stickers are some of the ways! You don't have to use the stickers just as they are. Feel free to adjust the size, color, or shape of them, as you wish. Fold a stage set for your art, or a small booklet or album, or a folded pocket.

From simple to complex, a folded object offers great fascination. In this chapter we offer many wonderful folded-paper craft projects. In other projects in this chapter, we have enhanced or altered the color of a sticker before using it in a project. And then there are projects in which we have cut and used portions of the stickers or the whole sticker rearranged!

We've learned the basics, and now it's time to push ahead. This is fun. We love folded cards and mini-albums, and booklets and albums with pockets. We've folded them in as many shapes as possible—stars, in horizontal folds, one long page folded in alternate mountain and valley folds. We've folded small papers in half and glued each back-to-back with an identical sheet and repeated this until

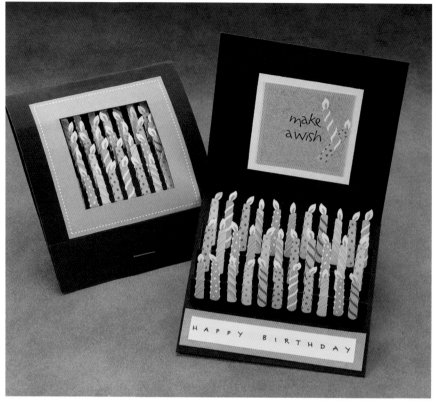

we filled a small booklet. We've created gift pocket cards or albums. We even have a folded card with hands that clap when you open it. The die-cut hands are attached to alternate sides of the vertical mountain folds in the spine of the card. And then there are boxes and bags cut and folded to create sculptural pieces.

Stickers can be altered; they can be cut and colored. There is no reason not to enhance the color, or change it with colored pencils or paint or ink. Or even by adding a different paper accent to the sticker. And if you cut the sticker and use only a portion, save the rest for another time. Stickers are meant to be played with, and your imagination is the only thing to limit you. And who wants a limited imagination?

If you have a favorite design, there is no reason why you can't use it over and over again. Simply vary the background colors and arrangement to suit the occasion. Or change the color, shape, or size of the sticker itself. With a little creativity, you can change the sticker or the composition and see a whole range of possibilities.

Happy Birthday Candle Matchbooks

Three folded layers in a large matchbook-shape card are filled with birthday candle stickers to set the day off right. The multi-colored candles against the back background are dramatic scene stealers. When the card is closed the medium-blue frame complements the candle colors.

FOR BLUE-FRAME CARD:

1. Fold a 4 x 9 $^3/_4$-inch piece of black cardstock into a matchbook card, scoring paper at 4 $^1/_8$ inches and 8 $^5/_8$ inches from the top to create fold lines. Fold on the fold lines.

2. Staple the flap at the bottom of the card to the back cover creating closure. Be careful to staple near the bottom of the flap to allow the top to tuck inside the flap when the cover is closed. Cut a 2-inch square in the center of the front panel. Add a blue frame around the opening.

3. Cut five black cardstock strips using the template on page 127. Score and fold across the strip $^1/_8$ inch up from the bottom of the flap. Create five rows of twelve stickers, lightly powdering any exposed adhesive on the back to neutralize it. Align all the candle stickers at the bottom on the fold.

FOR THE OPEN CARD:

1. Create three rows of eleven candles aligned on folded black cardstock just as the blue-frame card.

2. Layer paper, mats, and caption stickers to create greeting panels inside card.

HEART CARD

A simple concept with delightful results. We cut nine three-sided flaps—three across and three deep, each ¾-inch square, ¼-inch apart—in the center of black cardstock cut to card size. Attach the black flapped cardstock to the front of the card. The flaps open from either the left or the right, as you wish. Write a special message or gift message on the white card, beneath each flap. Decorate the top side of each of the flaps with nine of the 25 Heart stickers. Messages here range from 'A Foot Massage" to "A Good Book," "A Walk on the Beach" to "A Romantic Evening." A lovely gift and card in one for a favorite person.

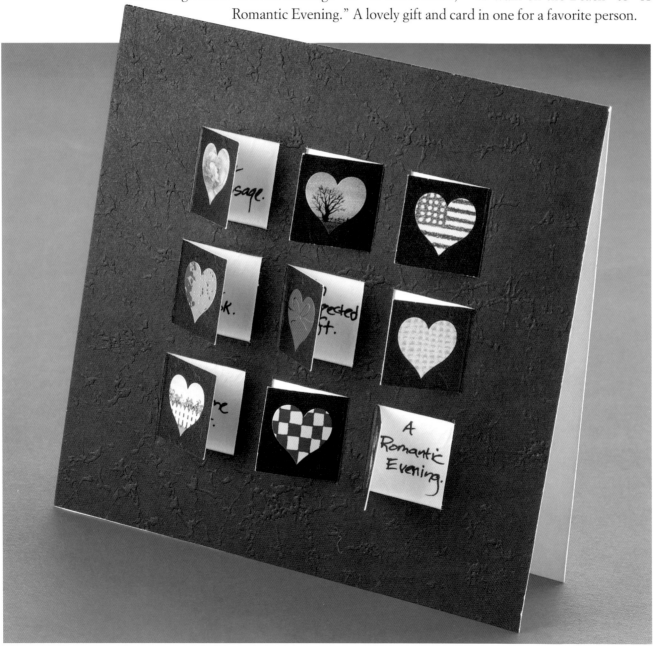

Lift-the-flaps cards are always fun and creative.

PLAN THE MESSAGES AHEAD OF TIME, AND PRACTICE WRITING THEM OUT IN THE ALLOTTED SPACE. THE ORGANIZATION AND RHYTHM OF THE CARD DESIGN SHOULD BE CONTINUED BENEATH THE FLAPS.

FISHING VEST

A whimsical card for the Dad who loves to fish will bring a smile. The fish diving into the vest pocket is a favorite of ours. Draw a vest shape out of khaki and light tan paper. Glue to card front, and cut the vest shape out of the double layer. Using a fine-tip black marker, add stitching marks to the front of the vest and each pocket. Decorate pockets with bait and "dad" stickers and attach to front of vest with small pieces of foam tape. Trim head off a fish sticker and tuck the fish upside-down behind Dad's left-hand pocket. Place button stickers down the front of the vest. Lay fishing pole sticker across front of vest, attaching sticker to front of Dad's left pocket and right chest pocket. Powder the back of the rest of sticker to keep it popped up from card surface.

POCKET CARD

This amusing dimensional tool-belt card will give Dad a laugh, and possibly a hint that his carpentry skills are valued! The palette is handsome and practical, the use of the tools as letterforms is a nice touch. Cover the lower edge of a tan card with ribbed red cardstock. Create a tool belt of tan cardstock and score at 1 ½ inches, 1 ¾ inches, 9 inches, and 9 ¼ inches and fold to create the dimensional pockets. Attach the belt to the card, as shown. Fill the pockets with sticker tools, some with foam tape to create a dimensional effect. Add finishing touches as shown.

MINI BABY ALBUM

We have folded paper as many ways as possible to create album pages. These mini-albums are some of our favorites. The interior pages are created from accordion-folding one 16 ½-inch length of cardstock. There is something magical about unfolding the pages and having small pictures of bright-eyed babies tumbling out. A few simple decorations are all you need to complete the album.

1. Score and fold a 3 x 6 ¼-inch piece of cardstock at 3 and 3 ¼ inches to create mini album cover.
2. Center a 3 x 2 1/4-inch piece of fabric on the spine. Edge with a coordinated color Design Line. Center fabric sticker block on textured paper cover and top with lamb sticker.
3. Accordion-fold a 16 ½-inch long x 2 ¾-inch high strip of cardstock into six 2 ¾-inch panels to create album pages. Fasten first and last panels to inside covers of album, threading a 12-inch length of narrow satin ribbon between cover and panel to create tie closure.
4. Trim edge of fabric-sheet spine with fabric Design Line border.

FABRIC-COVERED BABY ALBUM

Just when you thought it was safe to say you knew exactly what stickers were! Here are some embroidered stickers, made from fabric and applied like normal paper stickers. Are these not perfect to help celebrate the birth of a new baby? Pink, blue, and yellow embroidered tumbling baby blocks adorn a soft, soft pink and yellow fabric baby album cover. A pink and white gingham bow ties the pages together.

1. Wrap cover in pink and yellow polka dot fabric sheet.
2. Build frame from fabric Design Lines, ¼ inch from the outside edges of cover.
4. Center the embroidered baby patch inside the frame.

FOLDED-POCKET ENVELOPE

Create a folded-pocket envelope (cards with their own gift wrap) with bright-colored paper, printed or solid, for a special invitation—a Christmas tree-trimming party—or for a dinner invitation. We are concentrating here on the presentation of the card, on the special folded pocket. We wrapped the flat cards with colorful paper to create a pocket for them, gluing the pocket together at the back. Cut a sheet of paper slightly more than twice the width of your card, and a little taller. Center the card in the flat sheet and wrap the sheet around the card so that it meets and overlaps at the back. Determine the base line of the envelope, and fold the envelope at that base line up over the bottom edge of the card. To create a finished flap, unfold the bottom flaps and cut away the two outside panels beneath the bottom fold line. Then cut a diagonal line from the bottom of the remaining, middle, flap up and out to the outside edge of the base line.

VELLUM OVERLAY DINNER INVITATION

A delightful dinner-party invitation features silverware stickers visible through a porthole cut in the metallic vellum pocket envelope. The black and white invitation is simple and straightforward. A thin red ribbon around the envelope ties it all together.

Come to dinner!

Frank and Donna's house

Saturday, November 2nd

6:00 pm
Pasta, games and fun!

Regrets only 415 456-1055

Tree Trimming Party

December 18, 2005

7:30 pm

7 Pheasant Lane

Mia and Neil
201.924.4150

BY TUCKING A SIMPLE GOLD THREAD UNDER THE TOP OF EACH CHRISTMAS TREE ORNAMENT WE'VE ADDED DIMENSION TO THE PARTY INVITATION ENVELOPE. WE SECURED THE LOOSE ENDS WITH A SMALL GOLD BRAD.

TRI-FOLD BIRTHDAY CARD

The project is pretty, simple, and fun to create. Large vellum letters march across the bottom of the three folds to spell out BIRTHDAY while festive balloons float away off the top of the pages. "Happy" is a visual reminder on each panel. The Design Line borders anchor the edges of the pages. Use your imagination to change the components and the palette to change the look of the card.

1. Score fold a 6 x 7½-inch ivory cardstock rectangle into three sections 2 ½ inches apart. Cut ¾ inch off from the top of section 2 and 1 ½ inches from the top of section 3, to create ¾-inch steps.

2. Add sheer striped vellum Design Line stickers to the bottom edge of each panel. Add sheer vellum letters spelling "BIRTHDAY" aligning on the border sticker at the bottom of the panels as shown. Add a different color sheer stripe Design Line sticker across the top of the panels.

3. Add "happy" across the three panels. Add vellum balloons in primary colors and pastel colors. Powder the backs of the balloons lifting off the edges. Finish by adding sheer vellum streamers and confetti cut from color blocks, as shown.

Good wishes spring out of a folded card like laughter from a baby.

BIRTHDAY CARD

As one would expect, we have many creative staff members, and we celebrate birthdays. The staff creates cards for birthdays, each contributing a section or page, or some portion. The variations are wonderful. This celebratory folded card has a sophisticated metallic silver and black cover, and is closed with a silver ribbon. The interior pages—nine fold-out panels with a front and back, totaling eighteen individual pages—are full of warm wishes and naturally, fabulous stickers.

IF YOU ARE NOT BACKING THE METALLIC MATERIAL, CAREFULLY POWDER THE BACK BEFORE FOLDING, TO NEUTRALIZE THE ADHESIVE.

FOLDED DECORATIVE FANS

Accordion-folded metallic sheets developed into these exquisite Asian-inspired fans. Gold vellum Design Lines crisscross the small album cover, providing an interesting platform for the folded, popped fans. Back the metallic sheets with black cardstock to add weight, if necessary. The folding is very simple: accordion-fold the two-ply sheet (black-paper-backed metallic) from the left edge of the metallic paper. The undulating surface of the metallic paper reflects the light and creates drama. The fans popped off the surface increase the dimension and texture of the project. The intriguing details here are not only the fans, but the embellished handles on the fans. Vary the finishing step as you wish.

1. For the larger fan, cover a 7 ¹/₂ x 2 ¹/₂-inch piece of black paper with the same size piece of metallic sticker paper. For the smaller fan, start with 5 ¹/₂ x 2-inch pieces of black paper and metallic sticker sheet. Start accordion folding at the edge of the black-backed metallic piece. When completed, pinch together a ¹/₂-inch section at the base.

2. Wrap a thin strip of metallic sticker paper around the end of the larger fan to hold it together. Draw and cut a handle out of the same metallic sticker sheet. Remove liner and place over handle of smaller fan.

3. Add metallic nail head stickers to the handles. Finish by adding gold dots.

THEME AND VARIATIONS

As you can see, there is no reason to refrain from using a favorite technique or design over and over again. By making a few changes, some more subtle than others, you change the effect and feeling of the card. Selecting different color cardstocks is a first step, and then, of course, selecting different stickers makes a very big difference. We couldn't resist these fabulous variations on this pop-up technique. Here we have a clever "treemendous" thank-you card, a dramatic, colorful invitation to a garden tour, an uplifting note to friends who have moved away—"No Bones About It! we all miss you. . . the neighborhood has gone to the dogs," and an encouraging note for someone tackling a new job ("You should make a big splash!"). Have fun, and think of playing with images and words. Let your own personality shine through. And make the recipient smile.

CIRCUS, CIRCUS

Why not go all-out with an invitation to the circus? It doesn't happen very often! In this show-stopping birthday-party invitation, all the circus animals are poised, anticipating the arrival of the birthday boy and his guests. We have included a template to produce the pop-up arrangement, to help you create your own version.

1. Copy the template on page 128 to the appropriate size. Lay the template on top of the black cardstock. With a straight-edge ruler and an X-acto knife cut out the template on the cut (solid) lines. Then score the fold (dashed) lines with a bone folder. Remove the template and fold the scored lines with appropriate mountain and valley folds.

2. Pick up each animal, remembering that they will face out to the edges of the card, and add them to the individual supports. Note that the lion is sitting on a stand. Place the stand on the support first and then sit the lion on it. You might find it easier to pick up the animal stickers with tweezers.

3. Lightly powder the back side of each of the stickers once they are attached to the card. Blow the powder residue off the card with a light "puff." Add the heading and type panel. Decorate as room allows. Attach the cut and decorated black card stock to a large red card.

Pop-up cards are always magical. The surprise factor is essential.

HAPPY BIRTHDAY CARD

For a guaranteed cheer, try this ingenious accordion-folded card. The four rows of accordion pleats form the base to support hands that look to be clapping in celebration of a birthday as you open the card. What a wonderful idea for a birthday celebration, or congratulations for most any kind of accomplishment. And, once again, it is guaranteed to bring a smile.

Cut a blue strip of paper that measures 6 ¼ x 13 inches.

Fold at four inches from both ends to create the front and back covers. Decorate the front cover with a hand cut out that has been embellished with a cuff made from patterned paper and birthday-themed stickers. Tie a bow onto one of the fingers (with embroidery floss) to represent remembering the birthday. Accordion-fold the middle section, creating seven folds (each fold is ⅝ inch), resulting in a total of four accordion pleats, or rows.

Cut out twelve hands and add a cuff to each hand. We used an Ellison die-cut, but tracing your hand or your child's might be fun. Begin at the inside front cover and place one hand in each row, aligning the four hands. Attach the first four hands onto the front of each pleat. Attach the middle row onto the back side of each pleat. Attach the final four hands onto the front of each pleat. There needs to be a slight gap between each row of hands to prevent tangling as the card opens and closes. When the card is closed the hands sit straight up, but when the card is opened the hands form a criss crossing pattern that looks like they are clapping. Decorate the hands with colorful birthday-themed stickers. Finish the inside front and back covers with more stickers and handwritten greetings.

Another version of the intriguing accordion-folded card offers a dramatic night sky for all the astronomy-lovers you know. Use your imagination, and let your creativity flow. Sending a thank-you note for a lovely dinner, or weekend visit, or whatever, is not only thoughtful but generous when you offer your thanks with a handmade card. You are allowing the recipient to see into you and your life, your taste, humor, and style.

YOU ARE
OUT OF THIS WORLD

FOLDED ALBUM

A very simple tri-fold album with a pocket inside the front cover is just enough to record Lexi's tenth birthday celebration with family and friends. The album is simple to make and it would be fun to make one for each guest at the party. Include the little album with thank-you notes for the gifts, making sure, of course, to feature a photograph of the appropriate gift. Accordion-fold three panels and adorn each, front and back, with images of the party. The cover is cut a little larger to leave at least ¼ inch beyond the three outside edges of the interior pages. The pocket inside the front cover is just the place to store a longer journaling piece or a special memento from the birthday.

73

STAR FOLDING ALBUM

A festive New Year's Eve celebration is preserved in an appealing four-spread star book tied together with a gray silk ribbon. A pocket on one spread holds the dinner menus, while photos, firework decorations, and a journaled panel is on another. We adapted an Ellison template for this project. See the diagram on page 132. Fold an 8 1/2-inch square into quarters, remove the left bottom corner. Make a guide with a ruler and pencil. Cut from the bottom center fold to the center of the square. Fold the triangle in half with a mountain fold. Save two corner scraps for pockets. Cut out the tab from the bottom right square. Repeat this whole process three times to make four cards. Save leftover paper for journal panels. Apply glue to tab and adhere the center edge of the triangle to tab. Repeat on the three other cards. Stand up one card; coat the outside of the card with glue. Stand up a second card; line up and adhere the two cards together. Repeat, adding two more cards. For the pocket pages, tape down the ends of the ribbon to the inside cover. Glue the two edges of the triangle pocket and adhere to inside cover, hiding the ribbon.

BABY ALBUM

With soft washes of chalks or watercolors you can create stunning backgrounds for your sticker art, or even enhance the color of the stickers themselves. Use watercolor pencils and water to add more detail to simple stickers. Or, as we have done with this mini baby album, add luminous color to the leaf sticker centered on the cover with Pearl Ex, a metallic powder pigment available in many colors.

First, accordion fold a 2 $^3/_4$ x 10 $^1/_2$-inch piece of pink cardstock into four 2 $^1/_2$-inch wide sections. Place a green Design Line on each fold. Dab Versamark or any clear ink on the laser-cut leaf stickers and dust them with a combination of gold and copper Pearl Ex while stickers are still on the liner paper. Spray leaves with matte fixative. Center 1-inch vellum blocks on 1 $^5/_8$-inch squares of yellow paper. Add leaf stickers. Attach the paper panels to card, alternating with cropped photos. We alternated baby pictures with color-enhanced leaves, but you could use this idea and decorate the pages as you like.

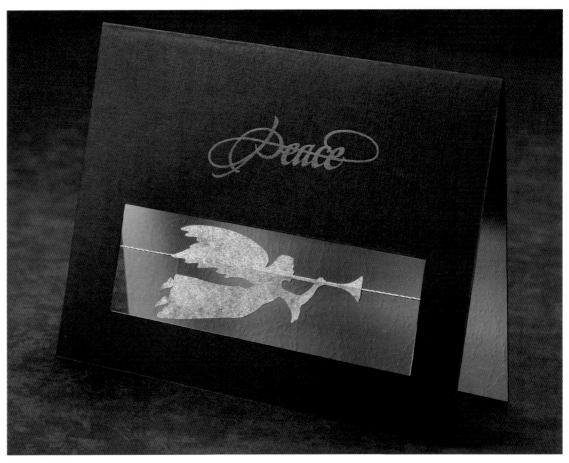

Changing a sticker color changes its effect.

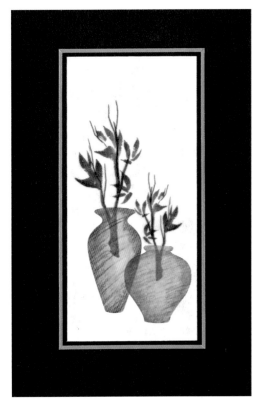

FLYING ANGEL

A window card can be simple and elegant. This metallic trumpeting angel stretches across the window—a mirror image fastened back-to-back on a taut, gold wire. She swivels as you lift open the card, revealing herself the same on both sides. The card is lined after you place the backed angel on the wire in the window (to cover the wire). The Peace greeting is covered with a metallic green pigment ink, covered with gold, copper, and bronze Pearl Ex pigment powder, and then sprayed with matte fixative.

PAINTED VASES

We used watercolor pencils to create the stunning color vases while the vellum stickers were still on the liner paper. Lightly brush the surface of the colored stickers with a damp paint brush or cotton swab to blend the color. When the stickers are dry, place the brushstroke branches on a 2 1/8 x 4 3/8-inch panel of ivory cardstock. Then, place the vases on top of the bottom portion of the branches. Center the ivory panel on the front of a black card, and frame the panel with narrow silver Design Lines, leaving a narrow black margin between the edge of the panel and the frame.

DRAMATIC COLOR

You can create quick silhouettes by inking a sticker. The palm tree stickers used for this card were green to start. We changed their color, and the effect. The metallic paper background is exotic, with end-of-day island light. The torn-paper waves increase the drama. Press a black ink pad over the stickers on the liner paper, making sure the coverage is solid.

1. Cover a 3 ⅝ x 5 ½-inch panel of cardstock with a metallic sheet.
2. Tear remaining pieces of the sheet into long narrow strips and layer across the bottom edge of the panel to create waves.
3. Coat three palm tree stickers on their liner paper with permanent black marker or permanent dye ink. When the ink is dry, place palm trees on the metallic panel with the edges of the trees off the edge of the panel. Trim away the portions of the stickers that are hanging off the edge.
4. Frame panel with narrow blue Design Line stickers.
5. Add message across the top of the panel.
6. Fold pale-pink cardstock to a 4 ⅝ x 6 ½-inch card. and center a 4 ¼ x 6 ¼-inch piece of pink vellum on top.
7. Attach decorated metallic panel to the top of the card with small pieces of foam tape.

♥

BE SURE TO TEST THE INK AND PAINT APPLICATION ON A SAMPLE STICKER BEFORE STARTING YOUR PROJECT TO MAKE SURE YOUR MATERIAL IS INK- OR PAINT-FRIENDLY AND TO GAGE THE AMOUNT OF INK YOU WILL NEED FOR THE COVERAGE YOU WANT.

♥

PAINTED LEAVES

These handsome placecards were for a special luncheon table. The place cards were made on gold cardstock with embellishments of wine and green cardstock adorned with color-enhanced laser-cut leaf stickers. The gold cardstock is folded with a tent fold, and the guest's name handwritten in beautiful calligraphy on both sides of the tent fold. (A great help to the guests sitting opposite each individual.) The color of the cardstock bearing the color-enhanced leaf signaled to the waiter the entrée choice the guest had pre-ordered. The color was applied to the leaves while they were still on the liner paper. First dab the sticker with Versamark or any clear ink, let dry, brush the surface with a combination of bronze and gold Pearl Ex pigment powder, and spray with matte fixative. The hand-colored leaves guaranteed that no two were exactly alike—just like real autumn leaves.

Andrea Grossman

Chuck Colson

CONFETTI GIFT BOX

We released a celebration of confetti by cutting the gift box open. The released confetti adds motion to the scene, and by hovering around the box, it keeps us focused on the gift itself—the focal point of the composition.

1. Layer vellum circles across a 2 ½ x 3-inch white cardstock rectangle.
2. Cut a 1-inch strip off the rectangle to create a box lid.
3. Wrap a ¼-inch-wide satin ribbon around the box lid and bottom.
4. Attach box and lid to front of card using small pieces of foam tape.
5. Attach satin ribbon bow to top of box with a small dot of glue.
6. Add the message and confetti squares as shown, placing stickers directly on the card, partially between the open lid and box.

STAR-FILLED GIFT BOX

Another sticker gift box, this time cut wide open, releases tissue paper and stars. The arrangement of the stars just above the open box confirms the focus of the composition. We can feel the motion of the released stars. While the sticker is still on liner paper, carefully cut across present sticker to create box lid and bottom. Pop the present bottom in the center of a flecked paper mat. Tuck a small folded square of iridescent cellophane into box using a small dot of glue to attach to paper panel. Stick box lid to panel.

Sprinkle gold stars above the package and tuck a few into the cellophane, as shown.

Add tiny gold accent dots with a paint pen.

THE BIG THRILL

Place an 8-inch section of the roller coaster Design Line sheet on black cardstock. Silhouette the mounted roller coaster and pop on the bottom edge of a 2 ¹/₂ x 8-inch panel of black cardstock with foam tape. Add fireworks above the roller coaster. Attach the black panel to the front of

A SECOND CHANCE

It's always fun to look beyond the image in front of you. Sometimes you don't need a whole sticker image. Cut roller-coaster stickers colorfully decorate the letters of the word "THANKS." Place the long roller-coaster sticker sheet onto white cardstock, and then die-cut the letters out of the layered paper. Easy, imaginative, and fun!

CHRISTMAS GIFT CARD

Tiny unusual-colored Christmas ornaments adorn this Christmas gift wallet card. The cool, soothing blue, purple, and green, not the obvious colors associated with the Christmas holiday season, make a strong impression. The large, delicate snowflakes cut to meet the edges of the card add motion. Fold a light-blue 4 $\frac{1}{8}$ x 10 $\frac{3}{4}$-inch piece of cardstock in half to create a 4 $\frac{1}{8}$ x 5 $\frac{3}{8}$-inch card. We used an Ellison die-cut to make this pocket card. Fold left and bottom edges of pocket to form flaps and attach to card. Line the back panel of the pocket with patterned paper as shown. Layer paper panels and decorate with stickers to create greeting. Cut and sprinkle snowflake stickers across pocket front. Decorate the front of the card as you wish.

MEDIEVAL CASTLE BOX

Do you have a youngster in your life interested in the Middle Ages? What a perfect gift box for a special occasion—their very own castle, complete with a radiant fireworks display! It almost wouldn't matter what was inside the box—almost. This idea could be adapted to become the cover of a school project. See beyond the specific projects; use the ideas and techniques.

NOEL CARD

Three large red and green patterned Christmas ball ornaments, back-to-back on a gold thread wind through the windows of a paneled, folded card. The palette is simple and consistent: alternate red and green panels, red and green ornaments, and red and green shadows on the gold letters support the gold stars and thread. Classic, simple, elegant.

1. We used an Ellison die-cut for this project. If you prefer to cut your own, cut red cardstock to 6 $\frac{1}{4}$ x 9 inches and punch two 2 $\frac{3}{4}$-inch square windows out of the center of the sheet, positioning each window 7/8 inch from the outside edge.

2. Cut two 2 $\frac{1}{4}$ x 6 $\frac{1}{4}$-inch strips of green cardstock and border right-hand edges with narrow gold vellum Design Line stickers. Attach green strips of paper to red paper, carefully cutting around window openings to create a green and red stripe pattern across surface of paper.

3. Die-cut or punch letters from gold metallic paper and back each with a red or green paper letter. Place across the bottom of the paper panel.

4. Back-to-back ornament stickers and string them across a piece of gold thread.

5. Back-to-back gold star stickers at each end of the thread and add additional stars as needed across the entire length.

6. Weave the thread of ornaments through windows and across paper panels, using small pieces of foam tape behind two or three stars to hold the embellishment in place.

VACATION CARD

An engaging dolphin swimming in the waves can remind the sender or the recipient of a rollicking beach vacation. Everything on this card says motion: the angle of the filmstrip, the breaking ocean waves, the diving dolphin, even the water drips around the title.

1. Place a 1 ¼ x 5 ½-inch piece of pale blue vellum in the center of a 1 ¾ x 5 ½-inch white cardstock panel.

2. Carefully place film strips on top of the paper panel, so that white paper shows through the sprocket holes of the film strip and blue vellum appears inside the frames.

3. Cut small sections of water from Ocean Design Line to fit into each frame of the filmstrip, aligning caps and foam on waves to create motion.

4. Cut dolphin stickers into pieces, separating tails and heads. Line up the cut edges of the dolphins with the edges of the wave stickers to create the illusion that the dolphins are playing in the waves.

5. Attach the completed filmstrip on the front of a 4 ½ x 6-inch blue card with small pieces of foam tape.

6. Place dolphin and camera stickers in bottom right corner.

7. Pop vacation sticker in upper left corner, placing splash stickers directly on surface of card to create dimension.

SEASCAPE ON SAND-COLORED CARD

A beautiful, matted beach scene looks difficult. Not so, with the Ocean Design Line sticker. Simply crop off a 3 ¾-inch section from the left edge of the sticker, place it on a vellum panel on a card, add a Design Line down the left side of the card, and embellish with a seashell and single glass accent.

SAND DOLLAR AND WAVESCAPE CARD IN VELLUM POCKET

We used a section of the same Ocean Design Line used for the card far right for this cool-toned blue seascape card in a vellum pocket. A silvery-blue sand dollar pull tag echoes the two on the vellum pocket.

SWIMMING PUGS CARD

Two chubby pups leading the life of Riley in their swimming pool, complete with inner tubes! We cut the pug stickers in half to sit them down into the inner tubes. Their back legs are under water (a torn vellum sheet) and their front legs are cut from their bodies and repositioned so they look like they are holding on to the inner tubes.

1. Tear the edge of a 2 ½ x 6 ¼-inch sheet of blue vellum and attach it along the bottom of a blue card. Leave the torn edge open. Cut the two pugs in half at their waists.

2. Tuck the rear legs under the torn edge of vellum. Use tweezers to easily slip the legs under the vellum.

3. Cut the front legs off the pugs. Working on sticker liner paper, build the scene. Place each pug top half in the inner tube opening. Add the front legs, positioned so they are holding on to the tube. Again, tweezers make the job cleaner.

4. When ready, add foam tape, dust with powder, and slip each completed scene on to the card above the appropriate set of legs! Add water drops to finish the scene.

EMBELLISHING

A simple recipe for success in creating any paper craft project is to choose a color scheme, create a balanced composition with a focal point and perspective, and add embellishments. The embellishments can be as simple as a mat or two of coordinating colors or as complex as multiple layers of folded papers, ribbons, eyelets, charms, etc. With sticker art, the embellishments could be eyelets or brads or ribbons, or even another sticker or two. And that is easy!

Who of us has not embellished a story to make it more interesting? Paper crafters embellish their pages or cards with decorative accents to "lift them up," to add style and visual interest. Selecting items to add to your cards, giftwrap, or album pages is a wonderfully creative prospect. Embellishments add color, weight, and texture to your sticker art projects.

You can create dazzling special effects just by adding surprising decorative embellishments to even the simplest design. We love to combine colors and textures that catch and reflect light from and off a variety of surfaces. Some send

shimmering colors in all directions, some capture and hold the color, some add shine, some add fibrous texture. Variety in shading, texture, and dimension add excitement to your artwork.

Decorative embellishments from sometimes-surprising sources can turn a simple sticker project into a stunning work of art. A recent explosion of decorative materials for paper crafters has produced an exciting assortment of fibers, metallic pieces, special paper products, buttons and bows that can turn your one-dimensional art into three-dimensional creative delights. You can select from mats, die-cuts, tags, fasteners, paper that has been folded, torn, cut, punched, quilled, woven, and pierced; buttons, beads, sequins, tiny jewels, additional stickers, three-dimensional foam tape or dots to lift items off the page, metallic brads, charms or eyelets, ribbon, yarn, or thread. And the list keeps growing. Look around you. If something appeals to you, try it. Think of the natural world as a source for embellishments—a flower or shell is always appropriate. And don't forget to have fun!

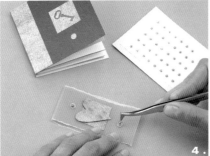

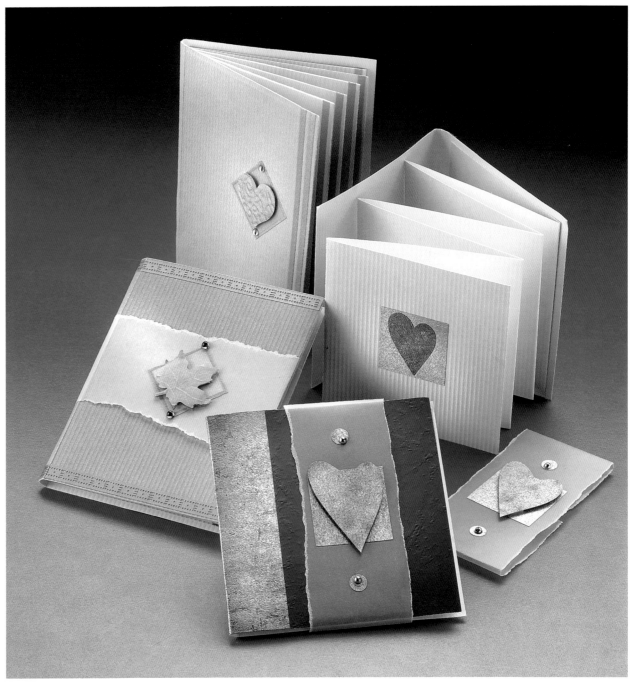

GIFT ALBUMS

A quartet of elegant small booklets/albums—some with a long single sheet accordion-folded to create the interior pages, others with individual sheets of trimmed paper glued back-to-back and then creased to create a two-page spread. The number of pages in each album ranges from six to ten. You can create an album with your specifications. Just adjust the spine of the cover to accommodate the bulk. The tall pink album in the rear is embellished with metallic Design Lines (on the edge of the cover and each page), a vellum square, and a metallic heart. The finishing touch on each of these books is the addition of two tiny gold or silver dot accents. We give you the technique and instructions specifically for creating the blue album. Please adjust the size and design to create an album you need.

1. Fold a 3 ¼ x 6 ¾-inch piece of dark blue paper 3 ¼ inches from the left and from the right edges to create the front cover. We placed a secret key on top of the metallic square, and a metallic dot above and below the square (which eventually will be covered with the decorated vellum band).

2. Wrap a metallic rectangle around the spine of the cover. Score and fold two 3 x 12-inch sheets of light blue paper every 3 inches to create an accordion. Glue the strips together, overlapping the first square, to create the pull out accordion book.

3. Attach the accordion pages to the inside back cover of the book. Embellish the inside pages of the book with complementary metallic blocks and hearts. Add photos or notes to personalize the book.

4. Tear the edges of a 2 ¼ x 7 ½-inch strip of blue vellum. Wrap the vellum around the closed book, overlapping and adhering the ends at the back. Repeat the cover composition on the vellum band. Center a metallic square, pop a large gold heart in the center of the square. Add a metallic dot above and below the square. Center a tiny gold dot accent in each metallic dot.

HEART SQUARES

A beautiful heart-shaped wreath of glorious flowers serves as the focal point for this card and small, wedding gift-photo album. The background papers are soft pink textured cardstock and pink vellum. The heart sticker is mounted on a square of pink cardstock and quartered. The four pieces are reassembled on a slightly larger square of vellum, leaving a small margin between each piece, and from there onto the card or album cover. The basic techniques are cutting and layering the heart wreath. Whatever would we do without digital cameras? The small, wedding gift-photo album was assembled quickly as a gift for the bride's attendants. Photos were added to prepared albums at the wedding!

SPECIAL TOUCHES

This collection of soft pink cards and and sage green album cover keeps summer in our days all year long. The layered album cover has a lovely little ribbon at the spine. A pearl-studded ribbon and tiny pearl corner-accents add textural decorative touches to the "you are special" card. The angled placement of the featured image makes us feel that this beautiful little envelope has been hung on the vellum just now, just for us! The angle adds graceful motion.

FOR THE "YOU ARE SPECIAL" CARD:

1. With a pencil and ruler, draw the envelope fold lines and flap on a 2 x 3-inch pink vellum rectangle. Attach to white cardstock panel the same size.

2. Cover the pencil lines with pink metallic Design Line stickers. Add the greeting.

3. Glue a 4-inch vellum square to a 4 ½-inch shell-pink card. Add foam tape to the back of the rose arrangement sticker, dust with baby powder, and add to the flap. Finish by adding a pink ribbon bow, decorated with tiny pearl accents. Attach the bow to the card at an angle, and hang the envelope (using tape on the back) from the ribbon strands. Four tiny pearl dots sit in the corners and a single popped rose embellishes the bottom right corner.

WHEN POPPING A DECORATIVE ORNAMENT, WE OFTEN PLACE THE STICKER ORNAMENT ON THE CARD AND THEN PLACE ANOTHER OF THE SAME STICKER ON TOP OF THE FIRST ONE USING MOUNTING TAPE TO LIFT THE TOP IMAGE OFF THE PAGE.

DRAGONFLY IN SUMMER

Every garden needs a dragonfly, and ours is no exception. The content is lovely, but this card is about texture and tone. Contrasting surfaces of two textured cardstocks and a vellum panel with a dominant off-center undulating torn edge are complimented by a stunning irregular-edged laser-cut medallion resting on the smooth vellum panel. The iridescent dragonfly deepens the palette and adds further contrast to the texture. The two-colored base contributes a sense of motion and energy to the card. No wonder this is a favorite.

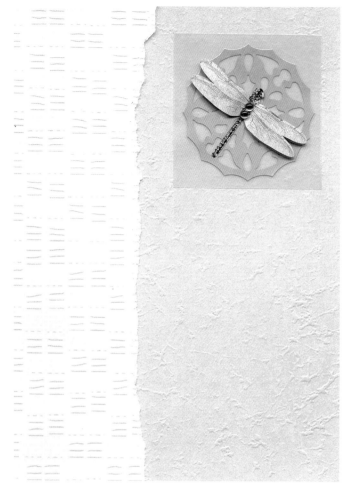

TRIO OF HEARTS

Pale yellow textured cardstock offers an elegant platform for this gentle card. Multiple textures and a beautifully coordinated palette make a quietly elegant statement. And yet there is an enormous amount of energy present. Each layer builds on the next: the panels are successively smaller, the texture changes subtlely, pulling us directly to the focal point of the three overlapping metallic hearts wrapped in gold thread. A tiny crystal gem adorns the smallest heart. What an expression of love.

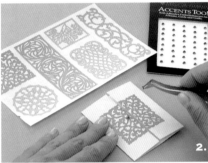

CLASSIC FLOURISH GATEFOLD CARD

The exquisite, intricate-patterned, laser-cut stickers are dramatically presented on these unique cards. Each sits on a vellum balcony with a torn edge, wrapped with delicate fringed fibers. The laser-cut stickers are mounted on a coordinated cardstock and then cut in half to create a small center-opening card.

1. Score and fold a 3 x 5-inch strip of ivory cardstock at 1 ¼ inches and 3 ¾ inches to create a 2 ½-inch square card with a gatefold opening. While sticker is still on the liner paper, cut a square Classic Flourish medallion in half, cutting through the sticker backer paper

2. Peel off each half and stick down on each side of the gatefold opening. Add two gem doorknobs.

3. Tear top edge of a 6 x 4 ½-inch piece of ivory vellum and fold into a pocket using template on page 129. Wrap vellum pocket around the mounted Classic Flourish gatefold card; wrap with textiles, and attach to front of 4 ½ x 6 ½-inch black card. Tuck the card inside the vellum pocket.

A SAVVY TRIO

Wouldn't you love to receive a gift in one of these delightful small packages—a box, a bag, or a heart-filled pillow box? The possibilities for embellishing these gift packages are many. Choose your favorite colors or your favorite images and let your imagination and creativity fly. When you think of building a scene remember that negative space (the space between the images) is as strong a design element as the positive image itself. Give your images room to breathe, room to perform.

The box plaid was created with vellum Design Line stickers, a sticker frame, one dragonfly, and tiny glass accents. The pillow box is covered with vellum hearts and a big organza bow. And the small violet bag, constructed from tags, holds a spray of lavender with a decorated panel, and a white ribbon handle. We love to create special packages. And we love to receive them.

ASIAN-INSPIRED PACKAGES

Wrapped or unwrapped, small boxes are intriguing. These simple small boxes and bags are beautifully embellished with metallic stickers and shapes, as well as exquisite laser-cut panels. The unique packages are elegant gifts themselves. An arrangement of them on a table, desk, or shelf would enhance any décor. The weathered metallic sheen on the bags is complemented by the metallic panels and narrow metallic fibers and jewel accents. We've wrapped some of these boxes constructed using the templates on pages 125 and 130 to look like little bags, and we've left others unwrapped. The boxes can be handmade or purchased commercially. It is the embellishing that counts here! And stickers make embellishing so easy.

4TH OF JULY FESTIVITIES

A suite of sticker art projects for a 4th of July celebration range from an invitation to the party, a place card for the table, to a scrapbook page to remember the day. And what a memory! The local boatmen stage their own annual float parade on the water, and the results are as colorful as the participants! Lady Liberty watches over all, but this red, white, and blue bedecked Uncle Sam brings a smile to all. Black cardstock provides the base for each of the projects, trimmed to an appropriate dimension. Fireworks stickers surround the Statue of Liberty and explode across the pages. Silver accents embellish silver layered borders.

Celebration fireworks stickers are irresistible.

LAYERED METAL ON BLACK

A dramatic Asian-inspired card offers a subtle palette, an interesting arrangement of basic shapes, and intriguing texture. We have used three different textures with this card—smooth (the top piece with the brush stroke sticker on it), and embossed (the middle piece). The large piece with the torn edges on the bottom is a metallic sticker. Contrast is added with a silver dot adorning the crossed black strips, and a taupe glass square anchoring the edge of the smooth copper sheet.

Make a note card of black cardstock. Tear a copper metallic sticker sheet and attach it across the front of the card on a slight diagonal. Angle a small rectangle of silver embossed étal paper on the front of the card using foam tape or photo mounts. Place a brush stroke branch sticker on top of copper paper, and attach it angled off the top of the layers with foam tape. Criss-cross two thin strips of black cardstock across the front of the card. Add the amber square and silver dot to the card with bead tape, for a final flourish.

VELLUM BLOCKS

A long, slim card with three layered metallic vellum blocks is classically elegant. The subtle palette and soft texture of the vellum blocks are dramatically presented against the black background. The card is very simple to create. The colors can be layered in any order. Place three vellum metallic squares across the front of a black card. Layer three smaller squares in pleasing colors of descending size on top of each square. Center a crystal accent on each layered block. Wrap metallic thread around the folded edge of the card. The classically simple, centered composition makes a sophisticated statement. And, a special treat—the card can be presented in either a horizontal or vertical format.

ASIAN-INSPIRED BOXES

This stunning collection of small boxes is elegance personified. The boxes are not only wonderful to receive, but once you make one, you will be inspired to keep going. The combination of a subdued palette and geometric shapes with the tantalizing texture of the ribbons is irresistible. The photograph, at left, presents the consecutive steps to complete a gorgeous puzzle. The lavender box is made using the template on page 130. Center a metallic silver panel on the box top, cut two holes through the panel and box top, and run ribbon through the two holes. Wrap a band of a silver metallic sticker around the end of a drinking straw, and add a few narrow contrasting strips. Cut to create a bead. Place a silver panel on a decorative-edged square of the same paper as the box , and center a laser-cut medallion sticker on top. Cut a hole in the center, through the layers. Pull the ribbon ends together and through the laser panel. Slip the ends of the ribbon into the trimmed, decorated straw end/bead.

CHRISTMAS GIFTWRAP

Here are several options to consider when creating your own holiday packages. With or without ribbons, with or without paper, with or without bells, holiday cheer abounds with these bright packages and tags.

HAPPY BIRTHDAY TAGS

A bright, clean palette brings sunshine to any day, but particularly to a day of celebration. Tags of four different cool-toned colors are attached to one another, side-by-side, each bearing a warm yellow mat containing a vellum letter to spell out HAPPY BIRTHDAY. The tags are taped together from the back to form a banner that could stand on the festive table or be hung on the wall. The process is not difficult: each lavender letter sits on a yellow mat, each mat is mounted on a tag. The tags are adorned with iridescent "bubble" circle stickers and completed with a coordinating ribbon tied through a hole punched at the top of the tag.

TO INDICATE A FEELING OF MOTION, LIKE THESE BUBBLES, CUT SOME OF THE STICKER CIRCLES IN HALF AND LINE THE CUT EDGES UP WITH THE OUTSIDE EDGES OF TAGS.

Unique Surprises

We have seen the spectacular gift cards, album covers, scrapbook pages, giftwrap, and many other projects you can create with sticker art. Wait 'til you see what we have for you now! (And we have hardly started.) With luck, there will be some eye-opening projects that will get you thinking beyond the box, or beyond the card or album. We want you to be outrageous with your stickers. How about a special TicTacToe game with a sports theme for the athletic youngsters, or a heart theme for those so inclined? One of our favorite projects is a little plant embellished with back-to-back butterfly, dragonfly, and even a colorful snake stickers, or the delightful magnets (for the refrigerator, of course) made with Christmas cookie stickers, or the little ABC book, Counting book, and a small milk carton, matchbook covers, and our embroidered stickers on infant T-shirts and Onesies. We've cut and trimmed and embellished bright-color paper bags to create hand puppets and party bags. Why not offer little Halloween trick-or-treat bags of stickers this year instead of candy? We have gone to town. And we do have a lot of favorites!

But we keep coming back to some of our most special projects. Birthdays are all celebrated in style at Mrs. Grossman's. And we have included some of the delightful birthday cards made *by* staff members *for* staff members. Someone takes responsibility for each card; the components are handed out to the participants, and creativity reigns. They are treasures to keep and revisit again and again.

Some sticker artists pushed on to greater heights, even to fabulous constructed heights. One—a fabulous snowtown—was the result of a contest held a few years back. The winning sticker project is a dimensional alpine winter town with penguins skating, and frogs skiing, and dogs playing in the decorated-for-Christmas town. Another winter scene—penguins relaxing in Antarctica—is yet another contest winner. Other favorites were made, just for fun, by a Mrs. Grossman's staff member. These projects take dedication way beyond what most of us will have. But it's fun to see the extremes to which some sticker artists will go. And we love to see sticker artists of all levels being lifted up and encouraged by their artwork. Count your blessings; and celebrate life and all it has to offer.

ANDREA'S CARD

Beautiful color paper folded into a multi-paged booklet with openable windows on each page offers a variety of surfaces for well-wishers to send their greetings. Each spread is a different, harmonious-color paper; and each window opens to another harmonious-colored background. The design of the card is a simple centered window on layered pages, and messages and artwork are on the window flaps and in the windows! The colors are full of joy and celebration, the artwork whimsical and charming.

A STAR

When opened the card folds back like a star; one page on a flap to-be-opened adds excitement, and the cover is layered and cut.

KELLY'S CARD

Kelly's birthday card arrived in a small decorated box with one end attached to the inside box top and the other end to the inside box bottom. The accordion of good wishes rolls out as you open the box, each well-wisher taking a panel to send their messages. Each participant was given a 2 3/8-inch cardstock square (to fit into the box) with which to compose a message. Fifteen squares were then glued together in one long conga line, and folded into the box.

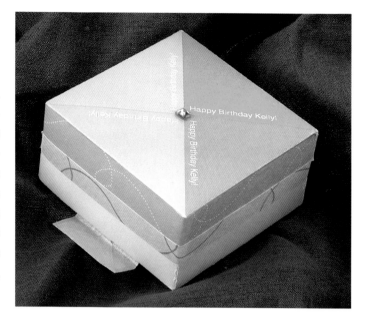

KEVIN'S CARD

For an adventurous cook, everyone jumped in and contributed a favorite chili pepper recipe. The very practical two-ring top binder book stands on the counter, ready for use. Every page is complete with sticker art and a recipe.

ARTICULATED SCARECROW

Ingenious pull-tabs and string techniques bring our cheerful sticker friends to life. An engineering degree is not required, but a little imagination is! The scarecrow can be mounted on a card or not. You might want to back the individual scarecrow stickers with cardstock for durability. Create the backdrop on the card using cornstalk stickers and a picket fence cut from woodgrain paper. Attach the arms and legs to the torso with tiny brads. Thread string along the back of the body, around the brad pins and around the arm and leg joints so that the parts move together. See the diagram on page 131.

Use small pieces of foam tape to attach the scarecrow to the card and support the head and torso.

ANDREA'S PAPER DOLL CARD

One might say this is taking birthday cards to the ultimate! Staff members created this card for Andrea Grossman. The participants were asked to dress one of the figures in a fold-up paper doll card made by one of the artists, using only stickers. The crew really turned themselves in. They decorated the paper dolls with expressions of themselves. Each of the participants signed their creations on the backs of the dolls, but they insisted that Andrea guess who made each figure. Word is that she did very well in linking the paper and real figures. Perhaps we do see ourselves as others see us. This is such a well-loved card, and such a fabuous expression of creativity, that it sits in a lucite box in the company library, and generates lots of smiles!

EACH OF THESE PAPER DOLLS WAS CREATED USING ONLY STICKERS. IF YOU LOOK CLOSELY, YOU'LL SEE PARTS OF BALLOONS, HEARTS, AND PLANTS MAKING UP THE CLOTHING, FACES, AND SHOES OF THESE DELIGHTFUL DOLLS.

DOG BONE CARD

No bones about it, good wishes flow from this birthday card, another staff invention! With as many as fifteen dogs at work on any given day, canines rule. They attend parties, meetings, and find their favorite "aunties" to take them out for a break. And it is all orderly, quiet, and wonderfully uplifting. No bones about it.

TOM COLLINS, ANYONE?

Blank vellum-covered cardstock discs were given to each participant with the instructions that one side of each circle would be an orange or lime slice; the other side was theirs to compose as they wished. The "envelope" would be a vellum "glass." The card arrived complete with straw.

AMY'S CARD

Amy loves jazz and rock. This perfect birthday card is a collection of handmade miniature record jackets and discs in a decorated box. Participants were given a small black "vinyl" disc and a "cover" to decorate for the collection.

DECORATIVE ITEMS

Once you start creating sticker art, you will find any number of objects to decorate. Having a dinner party? Embellish the candles on the dinner table with stickers. A birthday party? Spruce up the matchbooks you'll use to light the birthday candles. Having small party favors at the table? Enrich them with sticker art. Some of the projects are wonderfully simple, and take no more than five minutes to create. We have been known to bring a decorated box or book of matches with a hostess gift of candles. Whenever the recipients use them, they will think of you. And isn't that what you wanted?

TIC TAC TOE

When you have stickers on hand, you can make personalized versions of your favorite games. We have made a few tic-tac-toe games, and included a few sticker pairs as inspiration for gameboards you might like. We've used balls for a sports version, hearts for another, and black and white Scottie dogs. Nutcrackers or gingerbread men would make delightful holiday games. The steps for our Heart Tac Toe are in one photograph, below.

HEART TAC TOE

1. Stick hearts on a magnet sheet. You will need five each of two different stickers, for a total of ten playing pieces. Cut out each sticker. Place an identical new sticker over the cut-out one (this hides any errors made while cutting out magnet). Repeat for all playing pieces.

2. Apply a thick layer of 3D Crystal Lacquer (by Sakura Hobby Craft). Let dry. Repeat for all playing pieces.

3. Using a 4 ³/₄ x 7-inch magnet sheet, build the playing grid with nine 1 ³/₈-inch squares of black paper and the thinnest metallic Design Line (use double-sided tape or glue to adhere black paper squares to magnet sheet). Trim the playing grid with medium metallic Design Line. Using a craft knife and a sturdy ruler trim off any exposed magnet sheet from the sides and bottom of the game board if necessary.

4. Using the full sheet of metallic sticker, cover the rest of the exposed magnet sheet. Trim off any excess.

5. Add "Heart Tac Toe" and hearts to the top of the playing board.

POTTED PLANT

What a great birthday present! A small potted plant looks like it's sitting in a garden, full of iridescent butterflies, a dragonfly, assorted bugs, and even a snake, all back-to-back, on thin gold wire and stuck down into the plant.

107

ABC Book

What a perfect gift for the two-year old in your life. An ABC book made with stickers is just right for a toddler. This little book makes you want to have a two-year old around! The cover is a sticker-decorated, cheery red-and-white polka-dot fabric sticker sheet. The interior spreads, full of imagination, bright color, and whimsy, are enchanting. Not only is the sticker art unique, but the artist wrote the text in her own hand, making the book even more personal. This is a book to keep for a lifetime! Try your hand at making your own.

MY BOOK OF NUMBERS

We love creating projects for and with children, to see them excited about learning new things. Here we have a book of numbers for a toddler—as simple as can be. Colorful, simple sticker arrangements are visible behind a swinging numbered tag. Youngsters love reciting the numbers and specific items (birthday candles , ladybugs etc.) and swinging the numbered tag to reveal the colorful arrangements,

Layered and overlapped multiple color vellum numbers on the book's front cover hover around a central focal point, leaving lots of negative space around the outside edges.The book title in black alphabet letters is positioned on top of the colorful background.

MILK CARTON

A paper covered and decorated emptied small milk carton gets a new lease on life, this one with Easter candy. The square panels on all four sides of this carton are decorated for Easter, but adapt this design for any holiday for a unique package.

TEDDY BEAR ONESIE

A plush teddy bear ironed onto an infant onesie or T-shirt is a thoughtful gift. The adhesive is machine washable, but we recommend sewing a few stitches around the outside edge for long-term durability.

MAGNETIC MATERIAL IS NOT ALWAYS EASY TO CUT. PLACE ONE STICKER ON A SMALL PIECE OF MAGNET AND THEN SILHOUETTE THE SHAPE. ADD ANOTHER COPY OF THE SAME STICKER ON TOP OF THE SIL-HOUETTED MAGNET STICKER BEFORE COATING WITH 3-D CRYSTAL LACQUER TO ASSURE SMOOTH EDGES.

♥

LOVE BUG MAGNET STRIP

Build the filmstrip on an extra piece of liner paper, and place each frame on a strip of light blue vellum cut just wide enough to provide background for the image area. Let the sprockets holes be backed with white paper.

MAGNETS

This splendid little silver box with Christmas Cookie ornament magnets is a terrific Christmas stocking stuffer, or drop-off thinking-of-you small gift. Put the stickers on a black magnetic sheet. Silhouette, and place another sticker on top to hide any cutting flaws. Cover with 3-D Crystal Lacquer, and let dry. Decorate a small metallic box (Altoid boxes are favorites!) with ribbon stickers and a tag. The sticker magnets will stick inside!

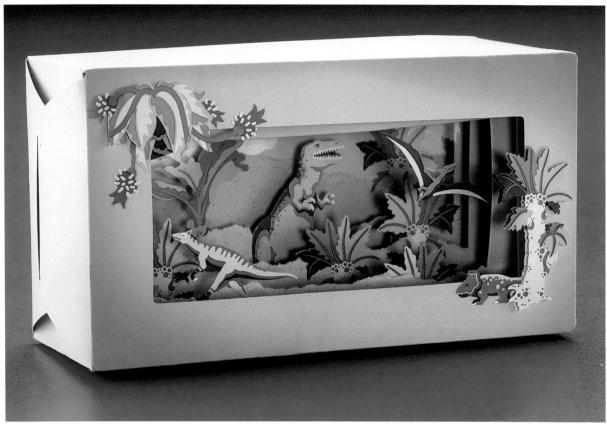

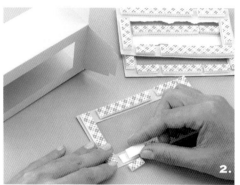

DINOSAUR DIORAMA

This wonderful window into time past is fun and instructive. You are making three windows and layering them vertically inside the box. It's like magic!

1. We used an Ellison die-cut to assemble the box. Tear the top edge of tan card-stock cut to fit inside the box. (We used 5 $\frac{1}{2}$ x 3 inches.) Glue the torn edge strip onto the back wall inside the box, creating a background of hills. Add jungle trees over the torn tan cardstock. Cut a piece of clear acetate slightly smaller than the outside frame measurement. Glue acetate to back of frame using a glue stick. Add stickers.

2. Make three frames with openings measuring 5 $\frac{1}{2}$ x 3 inches. Glue clear acetate windows to the back of each frame. Add three layers of foam tape to the backs of the three frames, over the acetate.

3. Make hills for each of the three frames by tearing the edges of three tan card-stock 1 $\frac{1}{2}$ x 5 $\frac{1}{2}$-inch strips at various heights so that when you layer the frames the hills are not blocking each other. Attach the tan strips to the front bottom of the frames. Build scenes for each of the windows with dinosaur and jungle stickers.

4. Decorate the outside of the box with cut and popped greenery in the top left corner, and a tiny dinosaur and tree in the lower right corner.

♥

STAGGER THE HEIGHTS OF THE TORN-EDGED HILLS ON THE FRAMES WHEN PREPARING THEM TO FIT INSIDE A DIARAMA. PLACE FROM THE SHORTEST IN FRONT TO THE TALLEST IN BACK.

♥

BAGS AND HAND-PUPPETS

Colorful, imaginative bags and hand puppets are created from bright colored gift bags and stickers (usually, parts of stickers). Projects guaranteed to delight youngsters, who may take part in making the bags for a birthday or Halloween party.

PEGASUS

The horse head is created from the template on page 131. Cut it from the top of a closed white bag so you are cutting both front and back of bag. Cut white paper for mane and tail, fringe the edges, and attach to the inside of the back section of the bag/head to create a mane. Cut ears and leg from excess pieces of white bag and attach inside folded or creased sides of bag. Fashion wings from a silver metallic sticker sheet, also cutting small detailed sections to attach to wing surface with small pieces of foam tape. Cut hoof, eye, nostril, and ear-lining pieces from silver metallic sticker sheet and attach to horse. Layer small opal confetti squares across pegasus' neck to create a garland. Embellish garland, eye, and wing with self-adhesive silver accents.

DOGGIE BAG

With a pencil, draw a curved line on the bag, about 3 3/8 inches up from the bottom of the bag, for the top of the dog's head. Trim off excess bag above the curved line with scissors. Cut a large rectangular piece of tan sticker sheet and mount to a white piece of paper. Then use templates on page 131 to cut out the muzzle and ears. Use an X-acto knife to cut the slit for a mouth. Use a template and black paper to make nose. Then attach to muzzle with foam tape. Make a tongue out of pink paper and slide top portion into the mouth. Attach on the backside of the muzzle with tape. Cut a small circle from the tan sticker sheet. Place on the bag. Use two blue dot stickers for eyes. Attach ears and muzzle with foam tape to finish.

BLACK CAT BAG

The black cat bag would be a delightful Halloween party bag. Use a pencil to draw the top of the cat's head on a small black bag. Then cut out with scissors. Place Candy Corn stickers inside the ears. Cut the pair of Cat Eye stickers in two and place. Cut three pieces of the purple Design Line, 2 3/4 inches long, and criss-cross them below the eyes. Cut Licorice sticker in half and place where mouth should be. Finish the cat by adhering a purple Jelly Bean sticker with foam tape for the nose.

GARDEN GREEN GOBLIN bag puppet

You'll need two green bags. Use a pencil to draw the goblin ears onto the smooth side of a green bag and cut out. Turn the second green bag upside down and attach goblin head to lower surface of bag. Lift the folded flap (the original bottom of the bag) and insert a large red heart for the mouth just under the edge. Cut the stems off sunflower stickers and use the blossoms as eyes. Cut arms from remaining pieces of a green bag and attach to the sides of the puppet, back-to-backing smaller sunflower stickers for hands. Run a Design Line border sticker along the bottom edge.

SPOTTED GIRAFFE

The giraffe is cut from an orange bag, and the head is constructed from excess scraps that were cut off to form the body. We used pinked-edge Design Lines for the mane, but you could create the edge of the mane with pinking shears yourself. Scatter various-sized dots across the giraffes's body to make his spots, and add small dots to make the face. We cut our dots from sticker balloons.

COLORFUL BAGS

These colorful paper bag "pets" look great sitting on a book shelf or table. Start with bright-colored small paper bags and cut and embellish your own critter. This is another imaginative project to create with a child.

WHAT REALLY GOES ON IN THE ANTARCTIC

ANTARCTICA

A winning entry from a sticker contest held several years ago. What really goes on in Antarctica, indeed. It looks like these fun-loving penguins have learned a few tricks from the tourists!

SNOWTOWN

This incredible contest-winning entry was made by a twenty-year old!

STICKER WORLD!

These four projects are beyond anything most of us would ever do, but they do show us that anything is possible with Mrs. Grossman's stickers and a creative imagination, an incredibly-detailed mind, and the patience of Job. Look at these with delight. No instructions!

ORGANIZATION IS KEY IF YOU WANT TO TACKLE A STICKER PROJECT OF THIS COMPLEXITY. SMALL VELLUM OR SEE-THROUGH ENVELOPES LABELED BY SUBJECT CAN SAVE TIME.

GREAT ADVENTURES PARK

Hilario Alcauter ran the laser-cutting machine for Mrs. Grossman's Paper Company for several years, and made many three-dimensional projects with laser-cut stickers, just for fun!

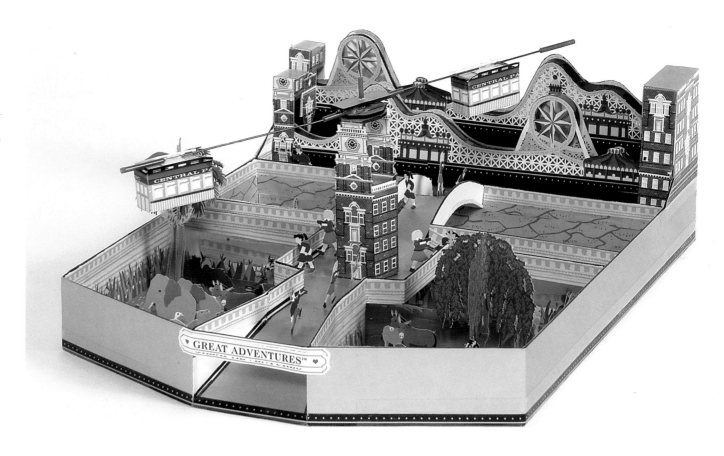

GREAT ADVENTURES CITY

Another Hilario Alcauter project with laser-cut stickers. Can you believe it?

ILLUSTRATED GLOSSARY OF STICKERS USED

You will need a supply of cardstock, vellum, and ribbons in addition to the stickers listed.

Some projects look like they require many stickers, but if you look at them you'll see that most are basic inventory and you will use them, and use them, and use them. They are: alphabets, blocks and panels in vellum, metal, fabric and papier, Design Lines (especially slivers), captions, flowers, and HEARTS!

♥ ♥ ♥

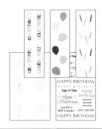

LAYERING & POPPING

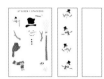

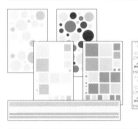
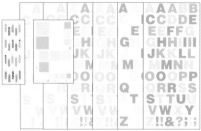
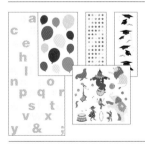
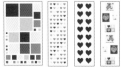

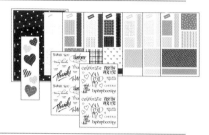
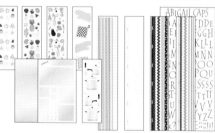
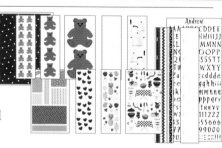

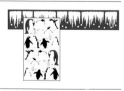

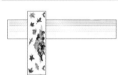
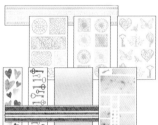
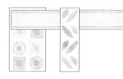

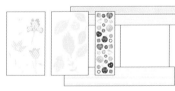
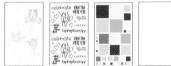

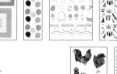

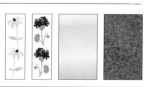

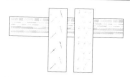

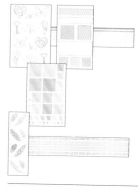

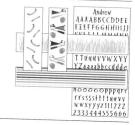

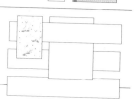

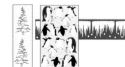
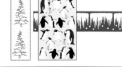

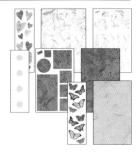
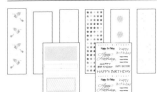

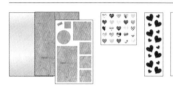

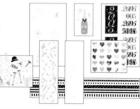

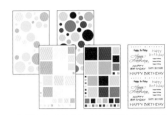

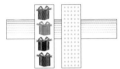

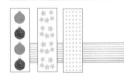

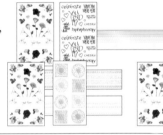

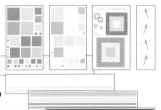

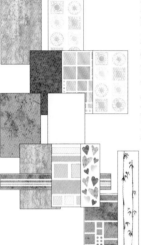
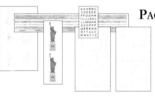

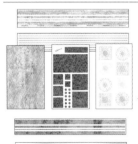

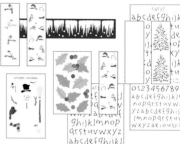

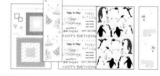

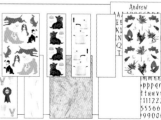

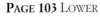
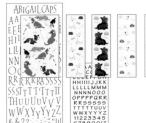
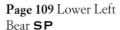
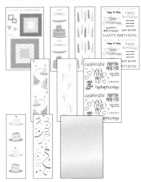

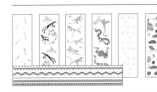
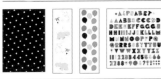

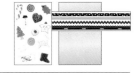

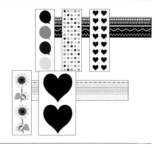
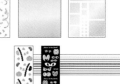

TEMPLATES

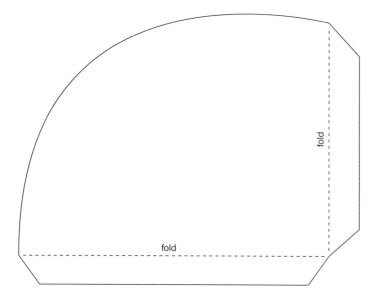

RECIPE BOOKLET POCKET TEMPLATE, PAGE 23
ENLARGE BY 165%

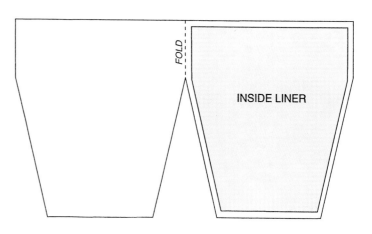

FOLD

INSIDE LINER

METALIC POT TEMPLATE, PAGE 34, TO SCALE

MATCHBOOK TEMPLATE, PAGE 92
ENLARGE BY 110%

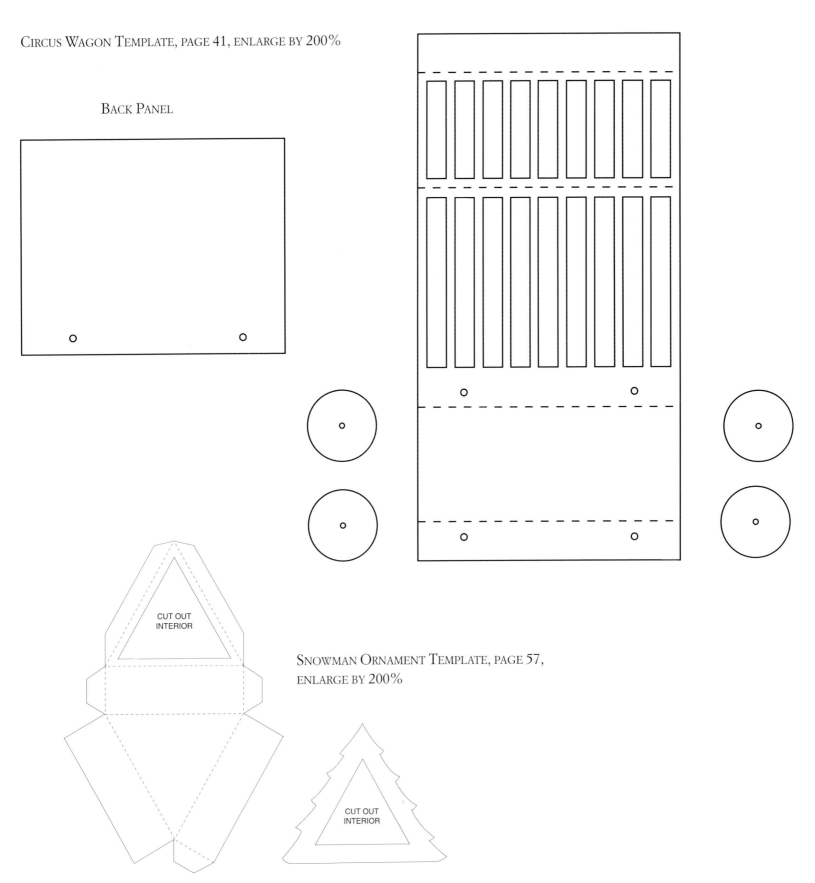

CIRCUS WAGON TEMPLATE, PAGE 41, ENLARGE BY 200%

BACK PANEL

CUT OUT
INTERIOR

SNOWMAN ORNAMENT TEMPLATE, PAGE 57,
ENLARGE BY 200%

CUT OUT
INTERIOR

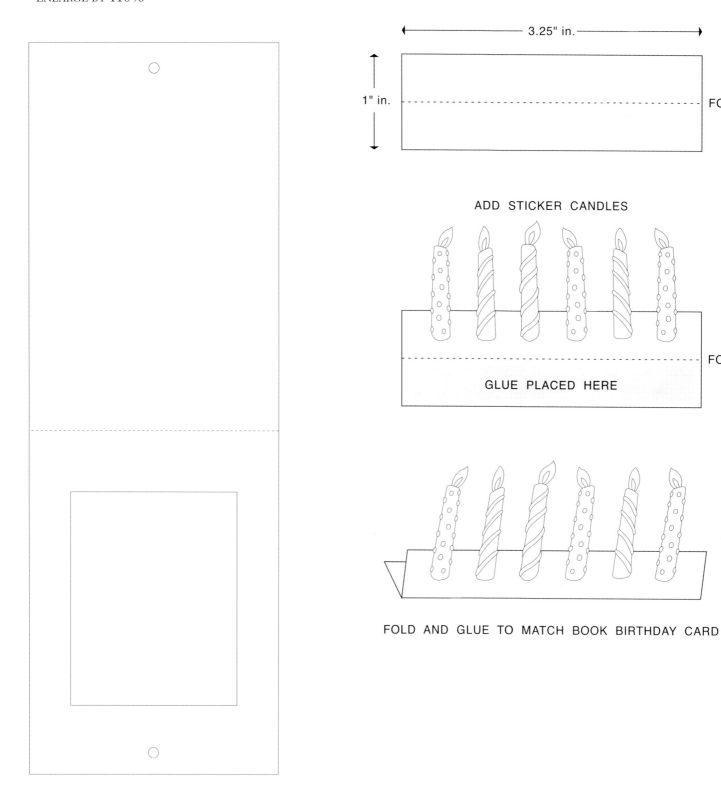

3.25" in.

1" in.

FOLD LINE

ADD STICKER CANDLES

FOLD LINE

GLUE PLACED HERE

FOLD AND GLUE TO MATCH BOOK BIRTHDAY CARD

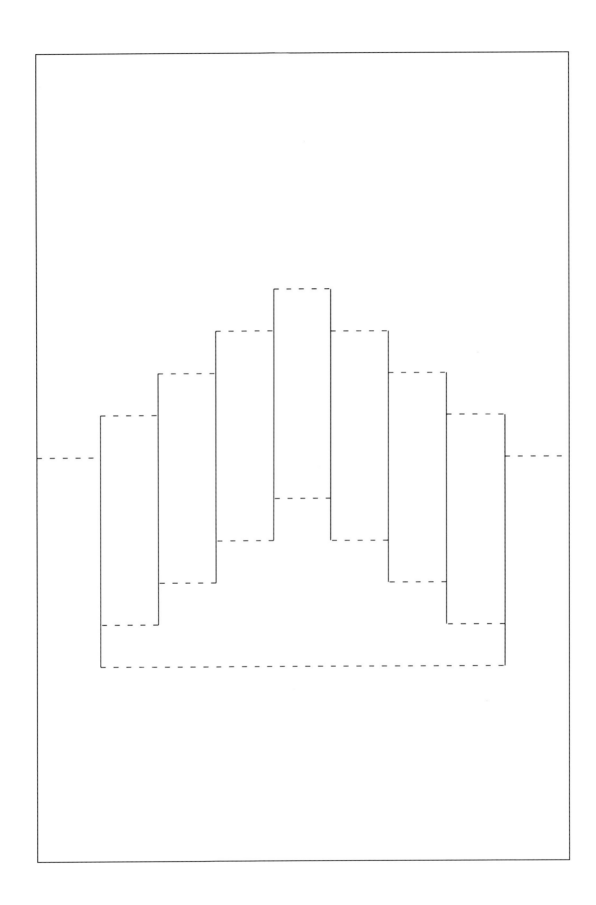

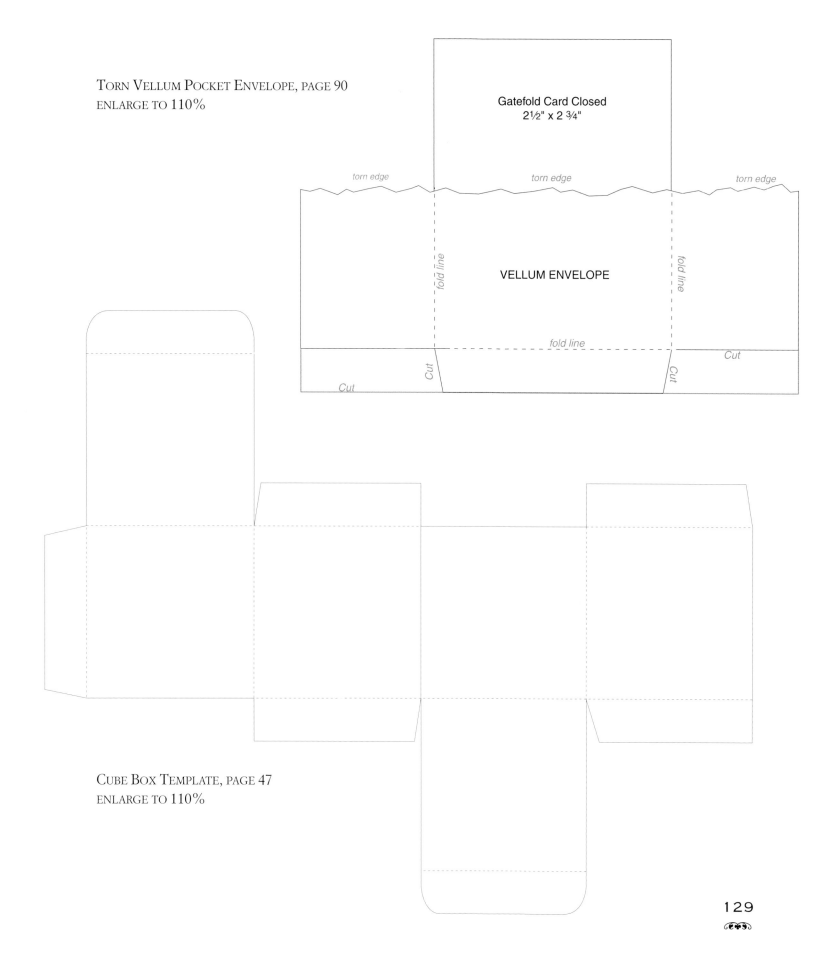

TORN VELLUM POCKET ENVELOPE, PAGE 90
ENLARGE TO 110%

Gatefold Card Closed
2½" x 2 ¾"

torn edge   torn edge   torn edge

fold line   fold line

VELLUM ENVELOPE

fold line

Cut   Cut

Cut   Cut

CUBE BOX TEMPLATE, PAGE 47
ENLARGE TO 110%

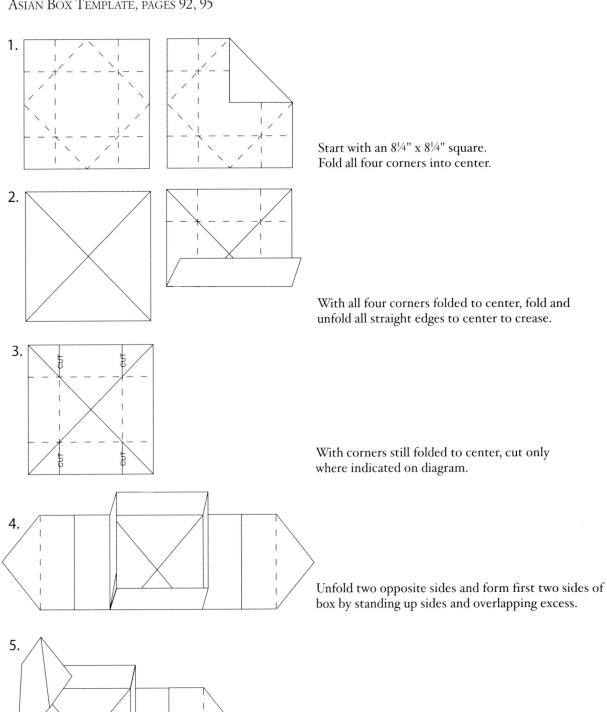

1. Start with an 8¼" x 8¼" square.
Fold all four corners into center.

2. With all four corners folded to center, fold and unfold all straight edges to center to crease.

3. With corners still folded to center, cut only where indicated on diagram.

4. Unfold two opposite sides and form first two sides of box by standing up sides and overlapping excess.

5. To secure box, fold remaining sides inward, over the existing sides and fasten to floor of box with a dab of glue stick.

6. Repeat steps 1-5 to make bottom of box using an 8" square of card stock.

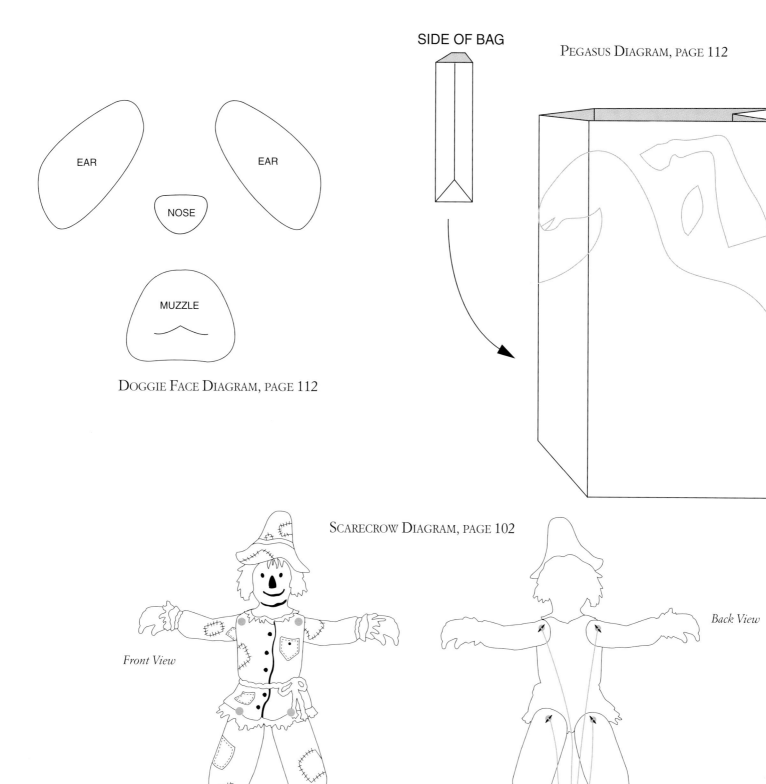

EAR

EAR

NOSE

MUZZLE

SIDE OF BAG

Pegasus Diagram, page 112

Doggie Face Diagram, page 112

Scarecrow Diagram, page 102

Front View

Back View

BRADS

KNOT

Cut solid lines
Fold dotted line

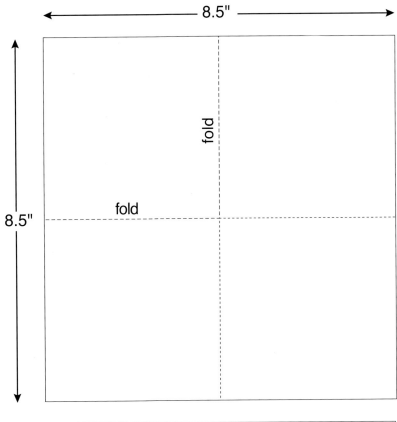

8.5"

8.5"

fold

fold

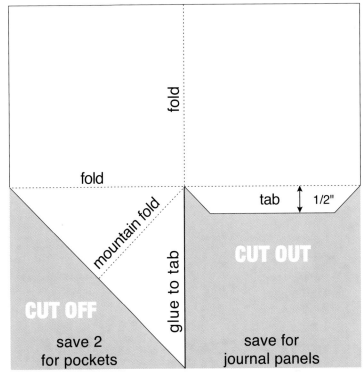

fold

fold

mountain fold

glue to tab

tab

1/2"

CUT OUT

CUT OFF

save 2
for pockets

save for
journal panels